Practical social work

Published in conjunction with
the British Association of Social Workers
Series Editor: Jo Campling

BASW

Social work is at an important stage in its development. The profession is facing fresh challenges to work flexibly in fast-changing social and organisational environments. New requirements for training are also demanding a more critical and reflective, as well as more highly skilled, approach to practice.

The British Association of Social Workers (www.basw.co.uk) has always been conscious of its role in setting guidelines for practice and in seeking to raise professional standards. The concept of the *Practical Social Work* series was conceived to fulfil a genuine professional need for a carefully planned, coherent series of texts that would stimulate and inform debate, thereby contributing to the development of practitioners' skills and professionalism.

Newly relaunched, the series continues to address the needs of all those who are looking to deepen and refresh their understanding and skills. It is designed for students and busy professionals alike. Each book marries practice issues and challenges with the latest theory and research in a compact and applied format. The authors represent a wide variety of experience both as educators and practitioners. Taken together, the books set a standard in their clarity, relevance and rigour.

A list of new and best-selling titles in this series follows overleaf. A comprehensive list of titles available in the series, and further details about individual books, can be found online at:
www.palgrave.com/socialworkpolicy/basw

Series standing order **ISBN 0–333–80313–2**

You can receive future titles in this series as they are published by placing a standing order. Please contact your bookseller or, in the case of difficulty, contact us at the address below with your name and address, the title of the series and the ISBN quoted above.

Customer Services Department, Macmillan Distribution Ltd, Houndmills, Basingstoke, Hampshire RG21 6XS, England

Practical social work series

New and best-selling titles

Youth work practice

Edited by

Tony Jeffs and Mark K. Smith

palgrave
macmillan

First published 2010 by
PALGRAVE MACMILLAN

Palgrave Macmillan in the UK is an imprint of Macmillan Publishers Limited,
registered in England, company number 785998, of Houndmills, Basingstoke,
Hampshire RG21 6XS.

Palgrave Macmillan in the US is a division of St Martin's Press LLC,
175 Fifth Avenue, New York, NY 10010.

Palgrave Macmillan is the global academic imprint of the above companies
and has companies and representatives throughout the world.

Palgrave® and Macmillan® are registered trademarks in the United States,
the United Kingdom, Europe and other countries.

ISBN-13: 978-0-230-54302-7

This book is printed on paper suitable for recycling and made from fully
managed and sustained forest sources. Logging, pulping and manufacturing
processes are expected to conform to the environmental regulations of the
country of origin.

A catalogue record for this book is available from the British Library.

A catalog record for this book is available from the Library of Congress.

10 9 8 7 6 5 4 3 2 1
19 18 17 16 15 14 13 12 11 10

Printed in China

Contents

Acknowledgements

We would obviously like to thank the contributors for their support and enthusiasm. We would also like to thank the Palgrave editorial team who have been remarkably patient with editors who have at times found it difficult to carve out the time to complete their side of the bargain. With regard to both groups we can only hope they are content with the final result.

We also want to thank *Youth and Policy* for allowing us to use parts of an article 'Valuing youth work' (Jeffs and Smith 2008).

Notes on contributors

Huw Blacker is a qualified youth and community worker who has worked with young homeless adults and youth offenders in a variety of settings. He has utilized a range of approaches from arts-based work to outdoor education. He has conducted ethnographic research into the experiences of residents living in a hostel setting and the practice of hostel support workers.

David Collander-Brown worked for many years as a detached worker in both the voluntary and statutory sector. He was a tutor at the YMCA George Williams College and is a qualified counsellor. He currently is a Professional Development manager in the Connexions service.

Dod Forrest is a youth worker in Aberdeen and member of the Rowan Group, University of Aberdeen.

Ruth Gilchrist is a Training and Development Officer with UK Youth. She is a member of the editorial board of the journal *Youth and Policy*.

Sean Harte is a youth worker in Middlesbrough currently undertaking post-graduate study at Durham University. He has been involved in a broad range of voluntary and statutory youth projects.

Tony Jeffs is an Honorary Lecturer, Durham University, and Visiting Tutor, Ruskin College, Oxford.

Gina McLeod is a qualified community development worker experienced in working with young women and school children/young people both in the UK and in the world. She is currently involved in the Extended Schools agenda and is also a Practice-Supervisor for the YMCA.

Gill Millar is a qualified youth and community worker who has worked in local authorities, voluntary organisations and Higher Education as a youth worker, manager, trainer and adviser.

Howard Nurden's full-time youth work experience straddles the secular and the spiritual. He has worked for the statutory youth services and in the voluntary sector over the last 20 years. He is currently Head of Youth and Children's Work for a national voluntary organisation, as well as working with youth workers in training.

Gill Patton is a Training Officer for a youth service in north east England. Her background is youth and community work and targeted sexual health work.

Carole Pugh is a qualified youth worker with experience in a wide range of settings. She has been involved in national research into street-based youth work and young people-centred evaluation. She is currently a Voice and Influence Co-ordinator for statutory youth service.

John Rose was, prior to his recent retirement, Head of Youth Strategy Branch, Department of Education, Children and Lifelong Learning, Welsh Assembly.

Heather Smith is a qualified youth worker and teacher. She has worked in youth projects, a special school, a further education college and in supported housing. She now runs the student referral unit in a large school in south London.

Mark K. Smith is the Rank Research Fellow and Tutor at the YMCA George Williams College, London.

A note on terms

In this book, we describe the work in various ways. Here we examine briefly some of the key terms.

Community work

Some community workers describe themselves as educators. Others may view themselves, first and foremost, as organizers (of groups and activities), or as animateurs and developers. As a result, community work can take very different forms. To limit confusion we focus on aim and 'client group'. Thus, community work can be approached as work that fosters peoples' commitment to their neighbours, and participation in, and development of, local, democratic forms of organisation.

Community learning and development

The notion of community learning and development has gained considerable currency in Scotland – replacing the term 'community education'. One important report describes it as a way of listening and of working with people. It continues: 'We define this as informal learning and social development work with individuals and groups in their communities. The aim of this work is to strengthen communities by improving people's knowledge, skills and confidence, organisational ability and resources' (Scottish Executive 2003). As such it overlaps significantly with the notion of informal education and youth work.

Informal education

Some see informal education as the learning that goes on in daily life. Others may view it as education flowing from the learning projects that we undertake for ourselves. Many view it as the learning that comes as part of being involved in youth and community organisations. Informal education can be all of these things. It is a process – a way of helping people to learn. For us, informal education works through, and is driven by, conversation; involves exploring and enlarging experience; and can take place in any setting (see Jeffs and Smith 2005).

Lifelong learning

Lifelong learning has become something of a catchphrase within UK policy debates post-1990. A commonsense starting point would be that it refers to the distribution of learning throughout a person's lifespan. It would, thus, include the learning associated with involvement in family life, formal education, clubs and groups, and work. However, in current policy usage it tends to refer to the learning of adults and is predominately associated with the development of skills for economic success. In this responsibility for developing learning opportunities for adults is increasingly seen as less a matter for the state than for individuals and employers. While there is talk of informal learning and informal education it is often poorly theorized and seen as something to 'progress' from.

Non-formal education

Some describe the process of youth work as non-formal education. In this view, informal education is the lifelong process in which people learn from everyday experience; and non-formal education is organized educational activity outside formal systems (Coombs and Ahmed 1974; Jeffs and Smith 1990). The distinction made is largely administrative. Formal education is linked with schools and training institutions; non-formal education is linked with community groups and other organisations; and informal education covers what is left, for example, interactions with friends, family and work colleagues. The problem here is that people often organize educational events as part of their everyday experience and so the lines blur rapidly.

Social pedagogy and social education

In Germany and some European countries youth work is often placed in the realm of social pedagogy and associated with social work. Social pedagogy is a perspective, 'including social action which aims to promote human welfare through child-rearing and education practices; and to prevent or ease social problems by providing people with the means to manage their own lives, and make changes in their circumstances' (Cannan et al. 1992). Originally, in the mid-1800s, the term was used for a way of thinking about schooling as education *for* community (or sociality). Hence, social pedagogy is sometimes translated as 'community education'. In North America it was talked of as 'social education' – and connected with many of John Dewey's concerns. In Britain social education has tended to be used rather more to describe the process of fostering personal development and achieving maturity. It has a more individualistic orientation and may not put 'sharing in a common life' at its core, although there has been a consistent emphasis on working with groups.

More recently there has been a revival of interest in the notion of social pedagogy in Britain as a way of making sense of the integration of different roles in the children's workforce. Some commentators have favoured the use of pedagogue (as in Scottish pedagogue or Danish pedagogue) (see Smith 1999, 2009).

1 | Introducing youth work

Tony Jeffs and Mark K. Smith

A lot of people call themselves 'youth workers'. They can be found in many settings – in churches and religious organisations, local voluntary groups and in large international movements such as the Young Men's Christian Association (YMCA), and scouting and guiding. Schools and colleges, prisons, large not-for-profit organisations and state-provided children's and young people services also host what they describe as 'youth work'. New forms and locations are appearing all the time, and organisational boundaries have shifted at some speed in many countries over the last few years. Yet much of this movement, although significant, can serve as a distraction by encouraging us to focus attention on the way youth work is organised and managed instead of looking to its core features and what it does. For that reason we focus on practice – the judgements, values, ideas and activities that have consistently served to give it a discrete identity (Carter *et al.* 1995: 3–5). We attend to the ways in which youth workers think, feel and act, and what informs such processes.

What is youth work?

For over 150 years, five elements have fused to delineate what we now know as youth work and to distinguish it from other welfare activities. It is distinctive only when all are present. Remove one and what is observed may possess a resemblance to, but is unquestionably not, youth work. The five are a focus on:–

Voluntary participation. The voluntary principle delineates youth work from almost all other services provided for this age group (Jeffs 2001: 156). Young people have, traditionally, been able to freely enter into relationships with youth workers and to end those relationships when they want. This has fundamental implications for the ways in which workers operate and the opportunities open to them. It encourages them to think and work in rather more dialogical ways (*op. cit.*); develop programmes

1

attractive to young people; and to go to the places where they are (see, also, Davies 2005). In an increasingly regulated world that offers young people fewer and fewer genuine opportunities to exercise judgement – as opposed to being invited to participate and 'be listened to' – the chance to voluntarily engage with a worker or agency is a rare opportunity for them to act as citizens, and to meet with others.

Education and welfare. Historically, youth work did not develop to simply 'keep people off the streets', offer activities or provide amusement. Many early clubs grew out of Sunday schools and ragged schools, institutions that placed great emphasis on offering welfare and educational provision for young people (Montague 1904). The rise of the welfare state and expansion of state education during the late nineteenth to early and mid-twentieth centuries eradicated the need for youth agencies to provide mainstream welfare and educational services. With developments and changes in state support mechanisms, and the identification of other needs, the pattern of welfare provision shifted – but remains a significant element of youth work. Contemporary examples of this include support groups, counselling, careers advice and information and advice services relating to areas such as sexual health and housing. However, during the course of all these changes learning from being part of group life remained a key element. Over time the recognition of the value and importance of such learning was further enhanced as workers incorporated ideas and modes of practice developed to deepen practice not only within youth work but also within adult education and community work. Informal education (Brew 1946), social education (most notably Davies and Gibson 1967), experiential learning (Kolb 1976) and, more recently, social pedagogy are examples here. Each of these traditions encourages us to focus on learning through conversation, experience and relationship (see Jeffs and Smith 2005).

Young people. Although there have been shifts in age boundaries, youth work remains an age-specific activity. In Wales, for example, this is defined by a recent government strategy document as 11–25 years (Welsh Assembly Government 2007). While there may be problems around how we talk about and define youth – and around the sorts of expertise those working with young people can claim – there can be no doubting that many young people both view their experiences as being different to other age groups and seek out each other's company (Savage 2007). Youth workers have traditionally responded to this – and learnt to tap into the ways of understanding the world young people occupy and the nuances of youth cultures.

Association, relationship and community. 'Building relationships' has been central to both the rhetoric and practice of much youth work.

Relationships are seen as a fundamental source of learning and of happiness. The aim is to work with young people in community so that they might better relate to themselves, others and the world. Those within religious settings might well add in relationship to God. Association – joining together in companionship or to undertake some task, and the educative power of playing one's part in a group or association (Doyle and Smith 1999: 44) – has been part of working with young people from early on and was articulated in the Albemarle Report. It argued that encouraging 'young people to come together into groups of their own choosing is the fundamental task of the Service' (Ministry of Education 1960: 52). Historically, group work – the ability to enter, engage with and develop various types of social collectivities – was viewed as the central skill required of a youth worker (see, for example, Coyle 1948; Matthews 1966; Button 1974; Robertson 2005; Newman and Robertson 2006). Youth work is fundamentally about community; about working, as John Dewey (1916) put it, so that all may share in the common life. It is an activity of communities.

Being friendly, accessible and responsive while acting with integrity. Youth work has come to be characterised by a belief that workers should not only be approachable and friendly, but they should also have faith in people and seek to live good lives. In other words, the person or character of the worker is of fundamental importance. As Basil Henriques put it (1933: 60): 'However much self-government in the club may be emphasised, the success of the club depends upon the personality and ingenuity of the leader.' The head of the club, he continued, must 'get to know and to understand really well every individual member. He must have it felt that he is their friend and servant' (*ibid.*: 61). Or as Josephine Macalister Brew (1957: 112–113) put it, 'young people want to know where they are and they need the friendship of those who have confidence and faith.' The settings workers help to build should be convivial; the relationships they form should be honest and characterised by 'give and take'; and the programmes they are involved in should be flexible (Hirsch 2005).

When thinking about these five elements it is also important to recognise the context in which they were forged. Since its inception youth work has overwhelmingly been undertaken by volunteers and workers operating in the context of local groups and clubs. These groups, in turn, are often part of national and international movements. Scouting and guiding provide a very visible and constant example of this. Youth work was born, and remains fundamentally a part, of civil society – that space located betwixt the realms of the state and the market, wherein individuals and collectives seek to serve and provide for other citizens. Civil society is the domain of religious organisation, family and, above all else, the voluntary association that allows citizens, as opposed to consumers, customers and clients, to exercise their freedom and through voluntary endeavour give expression to the deeper meanings of citizenship. In Ireland where youth work is defined in law, this is recognised. It is to be provided 'primarily by voluntary youth work organizations' (Government of Ireland 2001; see also Devlin 2008). The more the state becomes involved in the detail of youth work and seeks to direct practice, the more it risks destroying the work and the benefits it brings (Jeffs and Smith 2008). As Benjamin Barber explains, it is within the realms of civil society that we can find the alternatives to 'government gargantuanism and either market greed or identitarian parochialism' (1998: 44). Voluntary youth work for approaching two centuries has been one of those 'alternatives' serving and validating the intrinsic worth of civil society and the public domain.

The long trail of history and the dominance of the voluntary sector are often overlooked. Much contemporary comment is focused on the problems and travails of the statutory or state sector. The 'trade' press is enthralled by the Beadledom and bumbledom of state agencies seeking to micro-manage practice from afar via circulars, regulation and an unremitting flow of short-term funding initiatives and franchises. Yet, the broad-base of voluntary effort carries on regardless. As with the oft-cited iceberg, the greater part of the edifice still lies beneath the surface, and therefore all too often out of sight. It is crucial that due care and attention is paid to the voluntary sector. Partly this is necessary to focus attention upon the need to protect it from the backwash caused by the floundering of the state-sponsored work, but also so that practitioners do not become needlessly pessimistic regarding the future health and well-being of youth work.

It is doubtful if any other welfare sector now possesses anything approaching a similar balance between paid and voluntary workers. Health, social work, schooling and social housing are each dominated by professionals directly employed by the state or by agencies predominately reliant on central or local government funding and therefore dancing to the tune of their outcomes and outputs. This singular difference makes it far easier to be confident regarding the long-term survival and vibrancy of youth work as an activity. Voluntarism provides, over time, a cushion against the vagaries of state funding, the inconsistencies of policy and the negative impact of economic upheavals. It gifts a promise of continuity.

The benefits of youth work

Youth workers have rightly tended over the years to be suspicious of the quest for immediate outcome. As Brew (1957: 183) put it, 'A youth leader must try not to be too concerned about results, and at all costs not to be over-anxious.' Informal education and the forms of 'being there' for young people that are involved in youth groups and clubs are based, essentially, in hope and faith (see Doyle and Smith forthcoming; Halpin 2003a, 2003b). Such an orientation is more likely to find a home within religious and community organisations and groups than within the target-driven culture of state-sponsored provision and some trust-funded work. However, it is possible to identify the benefits of local youth work. These can be grouped around five main headings. Locally organised, community-based provision offers:

Sanctuary. A safe space away from the daily surveillance and pressures of families, schooling and street life is one of the fundamental elements of successful local youth organisations (see McLaughlin *et al.* 1994; Doyle and Smith forthcoming). Barton Hirsch (2005) found such organisations were attractive to young people in significant part as they provided a second home. They are often places where workers care and young people are valued, respected and have choice (Spence *et al.* 2007: 43). This is all the more significant as current policy concerns with 'joined-up services' and with monitoring young people are eroding such space within state-sponsored provision and, more generally, public space. The emphasis upon the collection of data within state-sponsored services discourages some young people, who are anxious to retain their privacy and autonomy, from engaging with workers. Almost certainly it results in others opting to avoid 'disclosure' on the justifiable grounds that what they say will not be treated as confidential. It also represents a major attack on the rights of young people. Three of the major databases affecting children and young people in England, for example – ContactPoint, the electronic Common Assessment Framework and ONSET – were found by the Joseph Rowntree Reform Trust to be 'almost certainly illegal under human rights or data protection law and should be scrapped or substantially redesigned' (Anderson *et al.* 2009: 5). Finally collecting and processing data severely erodes the time available to workers that can be devoted to face-to-face contact and the sustaining of relationships. Research indicates that in some projects even before the introduction of mass databasing between a fifth and a quarter of the workers designated time was devoted to handling data (Crimmens *et al.* 2004).

Enjoyable activity. This activity ranges from hanging about with friends through participation in arts and sports to organizing the group itself. As Spence *et al.* (2007: 134) concluded, 'It is the open informality of youth work which encourages the engagement of young people who refuse other institutional participation.' Ahmed *et al.* (2007: xi) similarly found that the young people in their study 'especially valued creative and informal approaches, which enabled them to have a say'. Studies of those participating in more open forms of youth work have consistently shown that young people particularly value the space for social interaction and for hanging about with friends and peers (earlier research includes Bone and Ross 1972; Department of Education and Science 1983). However, a significant number of young people seek out, welcome and benefit from involvement in more focused activities and the opportunities for enjoyment and development they offer (Feinstein *et al.* 2007). Structured programmes of activities are not without problems though. As Hirsch (2005: 135) found, they have the potential to diminish the quality of interpersonal relationships, and can lack fit with the culture of settings. When there is too much focus on what others judge to be what young people need to learn, it 'can easily turn into a deficit organisation, which is not what young people need or expect in these settings'.

Personal and social development. Social and personal development is seen as a core purpose for youth work by many commentators (see Merton *et al.* 2004). The annual reports of clubs and projects are often illustrated by little case studies of work or of changes in individuals; and the language of workers is full of references to personal development (see Brent 2004; Spence *et al.* 2007). However, for those using local groups opportunities for personal development are seen as an important aspect of their participation only by a small, but still significant, proportion (see, for example, Gillespie *et al.* 1992: 66–67). Assessing the impact of the work in this area is fraught with difficulties – and suffers from a certain amount of exaggeration where a target-driven culture dominates. However, there is evidence of personal and social development from reflective personal accounts (see, for example, Rose 1998: 127–133; Williamson 2004) and survey work and interviews (Merton *et al.* 2004). Merton *et al.*'s evaluation of youth work in England found that around two-thirds of young people in their survey claimed that youth work had made a considerable difference to their lives (2004: 46–51). The little long-term cohort research that we have confirms that involvement in uniformed groups, and church clubs and groups 'tend to be associated with positive adult outcomes' (Feinstein *et al.* 2007: 17). In contrast, this same research found that attendance at what were described as 'youth clubs' (defined as out-of-school-hours clubs for young people, 'typically run by local education authorities' but separate from schools (*op. cit.*: 6)) tended to have 'worse adult outcomes for many of the measures of adult social exclusion' (*op. cit.*: ii). This echoes the findings of research undertaken in the United States (Osgood *et al.* 1996) and Sweden (Mahoney *et al.* 2001) during the preceding decade. These results may well reflect, to a significant degree, the social background of those using these different forms of provision – but there could also be issues around the nature of the provision itself.

Relationship and community. Local groups and organisations provide settings where friendships and relationships of different kinds can flourish and grow. Central to this is the relationship between workers and young people. In terms of mentoring, neighbourhood-based youth work can compare well with other initiatives; 'the exceptionally large amount of time spent together, the willingness to have fun as well as educate, and the involvement of staff with the youth's family' all contribute (Hirsch 2005: 132). Furthermore, they are settings where young people 'connect with broader social institutions and the wider adult community' and provide non-familial settings in which 'societal rules for conduct are learned and integral to their emerging sense of self' (Hirsch 2005: 54). In other words, their associational nature helps to cultivate social capital and community (Smith 2001a; Robertson 2000, 2005).

Appreciation. Local activity involving local people is often better regarded by young people than provision linked to schools or state institutions. As McLaughlin *et al.* (1994: 5) found in their study of the role of neighbourhood organisations in the lives of 'inner city youth' in the USA, these were more likely to appreciate the realities of young people's lives and interests. Too often programmes and initiatives from 'outside' disappointed as they were 'developed by people unfamiliar with the daily rhythms, pressures and ferocity of the inner cities' (*op. cit.*).

The benefits associated with youth work based in civil society raise serious questions around the direction of many current policy preoccupations (Jeffs and Smith 2008). Youth work based in civil society tends to entail long-term, open-ended work defined by local needs and local people. They tend to look more to relationships and the enjoyment of each other's company (conviviality). Such work is also more communally focused and associational. Furthermore, those involved – both young people and workers – are often suspicious of state involvement, especially where it takes the form of specifying content and monitoring the individual young people involved.

The changing context

Sixty years ago overcrowding and the poor quality of the housing stock occupied by working-class families meant most young people were obliged to leave the house in order to undertake hobbies, meet friends and generally enjoy themselves. All but a tiny proportion were in full-time employment by the age of 15. In addition, many young men were conscripted into the armed forces 3 years later. At home young people usually shared unheated bedrooms with siblings, and the downstairs room with parents and not infrequently grandparents. The street was their playground with the youth club, cafe or dance-hall serving as a welcome refuge and alternative. Except at special times of the year the home was not often a place of entertainment nor somewhere to relax in comfort. Youth workers had a remit to work with these young people in their leisure time, to offer them informal and social education. Some sought them out in the streets (Paneth 1944; Goetschius and Tash 1967), others ran uniformed groups, many managed or worked in youth clubs that provided a range of activities and somewhere warm and welcoming where young people might gather and spend time with friends and friendly adults.

Buildings were then an essential feature of youth work. In urban areas it was not uncommon to find clubs that counted their membership in the hundreds (Jeffs 2005a). But irrespective of whether the young person lived in a rural, suburban or inner-city locale most had a variety of youth clubs, organisations or facilities they could affiliate to or casually engage with (see, for example, Reed 1950). Assumptions relating to the roles in society of men and women meant much youth work was single-sex and highly gendered, that workers and organisations alike operated according to long-standing beliefs as to what was, and was not, appropriate provision for a young man or a young woman. Therefore, a high proportion of the youth clubs were single-sex, likewise unformed groups, with the exception of the Woodcraft Folk (Davis 2000). There was no sign above the door of these clubs or huts mentioning that these agencies provided informal or social education but that was the underlying raison d'etre for their existence. Unambiguously many assumed their prime responsibility was to offer provision for those employed or in their final year of schooling. To provide those young people during the years of transition from school to employment, and from their parental to their married home, social and informal education, a safe place to meet and limited welfare provision relating to advice about careers, further education and relationships. They gave young people the opportunity to engage in group life and enjoy associational encounters that could draw them out of self-absorption and privatism and induct them into the grown-up amphitheatre of civil society. It was a service overwhelmingly provided by volunteers and paid part-timers for nationally the number of paid, full-time qualified youth workers was probably less than 1000 – far too few to offer anything more than a skeleton service.

As anyone reading the preceding paragraph will be aware during the course of the intervening years the situation it describes has changed radically. Take the home. It is now the norm for young people to have their own centrally heated room within which they will have a games console, television, 'music system' and, of course, a mobile phone. On average they spend around four and a half hours a day in front of a screen of some sort – more than they spend in a classroom and that spent with their parents. Significantly those living in the lowest income households are more likely to have their own television than their more prosperous peers (Mayo and Nairns 2009). Overall, as the home has become evermore the place of entertainment fewer and fewer young people spend time on the streets or public spaces (Valentine 2004). They have less need to do so in order to meet with friends (they see them at school and college and can be constant contact with via electronic mediums) and because they are discouraged from 'hanging out' by parents, the police and others (Measor and Squires 2000).

As the home has changed so has the relationship of young people with education and work. Within the lifetime of the grandparents of the present generation of young people the school-leaving age will have effectively risen from 14 to 18, and the proportion entering higher education immediately after completing their schooling risen tenfold. In the mid-1920s there were 29,275 (8376 of whom were women) studying at English universities (Mowat 1955); today there are over a million and a quarter over half of whom are women. Whereas approximately 80 per cent of young people entered work as soon as they legally were able to when the Albemarle Report was published 50 years ago, the figure now is in the region of 5 per cent. This lengthening of the process of transition to independence has had, and will continue to have, a profound impact.

With the overwhelming majority of young people in full-time education up to the age of 21 youth work intervention will increasingly be incorporated in, hosted or managed by educational institutions. Despite attempts to revive the free-standing youth club via initiatives such as *MyPlace*, the decline in the viability and number of such institutions that has been taking place for over 30 years is unlikely to decelerate. Not least because friendship networks will be overwhelmingly formed within education settings rather than neighbourhoods. Such a falling away also reflects demographic change – there are simply much lower concentrations of young people in most localities. This reflects in part the long-term fall in the birth-rate and a rise in life-expectancy. Now, for the first time, children and young people are outnumbered by those aged over 65.

Just as the re-drawing of the demographic profile will require a restructuring of youth work, so will social changes. The changing position of women in society, the shifting ethnic and cultural mix of the British population, the growing acceptance of gay and lesbian lifestyles, rising levels of economic inequality alongside growing affluence (Wilkinson and Pickett 2009), increasing levels of family breakdown and the weakening of community that has accompanied growing individualisation and the power of consumerism (see, for example, Sennett 2006; Barber 2007) have all impacted, and will continue to impact, on young people and youth work. These as well as economic and environmental challenges that are impossible to predict, along with technological advances in relation to digital communications, for example, that we can scarcely imagine (Loader 2007) will demand that agencies and practitioners must, like those who went before, be adaptable and responsive.

Changing policies and structures

For over a century in Britain what we now know as youth work flourished without significant state involvement. This situation changed in a matter of weeks following the outbreak of the Second World War in 1939. The era of 'total war' – with rationing, evacuation and bombing – created an urgent need for state funding and guidance to ensure universal provision (Jeffs 1979; Bradford 2009). Significantly, the British government was also desperate to avoid earlier models of state youth work established by totalitarian states such as Russia, Italy and Germany. At a time when the nation was locked into a struggle to sustain democracy it was essential that state youth work itself should foster democratic values and practices. Little or no innovation was needed here as there was a rich tradition of associational life, participation and democratic practice within many of the clubs and groups associated with churches, settlements and voluntary youth movements. Many of the established guides to practice (e.g., Henriques 1933) were quickly augmented by new texts that were self-consciously about youth work (most notably, Brew 1943; Rees 1943, 1944; Armson and Turnbull 1944). For these writers and others the role of the state was, predominately, to support what was occurring within civil society, augmenting provision where there were gaps and encouraging collaboration between agencies that had, in some cases, a history of mutual antagonism.

The model forged in the war years remained largely intact until the 1960s and 1970s. Indeed the last clear 'government' statements of youth work in its classic 'democratic' form can be found in the Albemarle Report (Ministry of Education 1960) and *Youth and Community Work in the 70s*, frequently referred to as the Fairbairn-Milson Report (Department of Education and Science 1969). The former famously talked about offering young people opportunities for association, training and challenge, the latter openings for participation, self-determination and political engagement. These documents now bear little meaningful relationship to contemporary state practice. With the fading away of the 'Cold War', the virtually unchecked progress of globalisation and the rise of market values and consumerism, successive governments have 'opted' to set different priorities. At the same time their ability to impose those priorities has increased markedly in many areas. This has been linked to the decline of key social and autonomous political movements and groups, and an enhanced capacity to monitor behaviour. In England documents such as *Every Child Matters* (H. M. Government 2003), *Transforming Youth Work* (Department for Education and Skills 2002) and *Youth Matters* (H. M. Government 2005), in Wales *Young People, Youth Work, Youth Service* (Welsh Assembly Government 2007) and in Scotland *Moving Forward* (Scottish Executive 2007) had none of the depth and rationale of their predecessors. They were simply prospectuses for the delivery of mostly already agreed priorities and policies. The twin priorities were public safety and economic productivity (and thus, private profit). The needs of the market came to dominate, and the well-being of civil society a matter of governmental indifference. Significantly, the one paper in recent years that had a fuller discussion and exploration, the English *Aiming High for Young People* (HM Treasury 2007) did not have youth work as its focus but rather 'positive activities' for young people.

Overall, current state policies around work with young people in Britain reflect a shift from voluntary participation to more coercive forms; from association to individualised activity; from education to case management; and from informal to formal and bureaucratic relationships (see Jeffs and Smith 2008). In England this process has been further exacerbated by the use of commissioning, and the development of integrated children's services and the disassembly of youth services within them. The effect has been a radical reshaping of work with young people within state-sponsored sectors. Instead of youth workers we more commonly find practitioners – with various titles – who lay claim to an expertise in working with, on and alongside young people. They are hired by agencies seeking to manage young people's behaviour and to promote 'positive transitions'. Within the English children's trust frameworks these workers often have new job titles like children and youth worker, youth development worker, youth support worker, social pedagogue and adolescent worker. Within schools and colleges they might have behaviour management, mentor or extended schooling in their titles.

A further twist came late in 2008 with the collapse of key elements of the global banking system, significant economic disruption and long-term pressure on government finances. Economic crisis and recession have historically pre-figured a sharp decline in central and local government investment in youth services and an equally marked fall in philanthropic support (Jeffs 1979). Rising unemployment and a shrinking tax-base inevitably lead to expenditure being focused on 'essential services' and a decline in the funds made available for marginal services such as youth work. The length and depth of recessions are obviously impossible to predict with any degree of precision; however, we can expect that what state funding is available will, for the coming decade, at least initially, be directed towards individualised work and targeted groups who threat to be 'socially disruptive'.

The way forward

The current shifting orientations in work with young people across Britain have, on the one hand, introduced constraints on the ability to engage in local, open and relational practice. On the other, the movements have opened up new spaces for exploration and engagement, and reopened some old ones – for example, within schools and further education colleges. There is, we believe, still room for groups of workers and for individuals within state-sponsored arenas to develop open, relational work with young people. Those operating firmly within civil society have considerable space for innovation and exploration – but face different issues. Here we want to highlight some of the opportunities and issues.

First, we have found that workers and managers generally impose boundaries on the work that are overcautious in terms of what might be possible in their situations. There are all sorts of reasons for this including the fear of being reprimanded, the desire for an easy life and the scale and complexity of the policies, procedures and paperwork that confront them. However, if we can get over these, there is often imprecision and slackness in systems and organisations that can be exploited to make space for more open and relational practice. For example, the lack of a management framework within some faith groups can be used to open up space for such practice. Similarly, the long line of reporting, the need in each layer of a bureaucracy to present its work in the best light and the amount of effort involved in channelling 'wayward' workers can also operate in the favour of those wanting to push and test boundaries (see Smith and Smith 2008).

Second, many of those working with young people have lost touch with, or not been introduced to, the rich tradition of thinking, practice and example that has developed within youth work (hence our focus here). The scope of training has been narrowed with diminished opportunities to study the historical origins and philosophical core under-pinning practice (Jeffs and Spence 2008). Newer generations of workers with young people have been increasingly socialised into defining their identity and activity around the narrowing concerns of the 'positive transitions' agenda, and more programmatic and outcome-oriented ways of working. Employer-controlled Foundation degrees and the expanding range of 'on-the-job routes to qualification' deliberately set out to lower horizons and replace education with training. While some may find comfort in these more formulaic approaches, many others, in our experience, find such ways of working unsatisfying and worrying. They seek the space wherein they can engage with young people in sustained and creative ways that place the emphasis on relationships and routes to informal educational encounters.

Third, there is increasing evidence that the dominant managerial orientation to social policy involving central target setting, and the delivery of services through a mix of state, non-profit and commercial operators is running itself into the ground. This can be seen, for example, in the developing debate around primary schooling (fuelled in part by the Esmée Fairbairn Foundation/Cambridge University *Primary Review*); the inability of the National Health Service to convert increased resources into a comparable improvement in health care (Wanless *et al.* 2007); and the growing opposition to excessive testing in secondary schools that has already led to reforms in Wales and Scotland. Just as the central planning model for economic policy fell apart in the late 1960s, now major cracks are appearing in the 'delivery' model for social policy that has dominated the last decade or so in the United Kingdom. Both state and business have failed to develop and provide social and educational services that actually address people's needs and aspirations. Policy for poor communities, and those deemed marginalised or disadvantaged:

> ...tends to be driven by a deficit model that focuses on the deficiencies of individuals and communities, rather than building upon the individual, associational, and institutional assets and networks that already exist.
>
> (Siranni and Friedland 2001: 11)

Schools, health and care providers can more easily plough on regardless of the damage they inflict. However, in the end deficit models of welfare and education fail. They cannot do what is necessary to effect lasting change. They do not engage with people in a meaningful way. Unfortunately, as John McKnight (1995: 106) has commented, 'As the power of profession and service system ascends, the legitimacy, authority, and capacity of citizens and community descend. The *citizen* retreats. The *client* advances.' The current situation in welfare and education has the look of a 'tipping point' – a moment when thinking and actions cross a threshold and rapid change occurs (Gladwell 2000).

Fourth, in the current context small disruptions to systems, micro-actions and locally improvised initiatives can bring about significant gains (Siranni and Friedland 2001; Speth 2005). We may well be approaching a moment when 'little things can make a big difference' (Gladwell 2000). By making the case for more open, local and relational ways of working, offering different examples of practice, and emphasizing the crucial significance of civil society, there is a chance of wider change. We know, for example, that when considering social innovation the most lasting and largest impacts are often not the result of organisational growth. Rather they 'come from encouraging emulators, and transforming how societies think (with new concepts, arguments and stories)' (Mulgan *et al.* 2007: iv).

In conclusion

As we have seen, in recent years the policy context in which youth work operates has been volatile and often incoherent. New agencies and funding streams appear and, often with equal rapidity, vanish. The funding structure has become chaotic and time consuming. As the Audit Commission found, around 28 per cent of staff time is now consumed writing bids for money and providing documentation for funders (2009: 76). Understandably, given this context, a certain despondency has infected state-sponsored youth work. Yet a lot remains that is vibrant and healthy and will undoubtedly survive and develop – much as youth work has weathered previous storms. Without adopting a sham optimism it is possible to rationally retain a faith in the buoyancy found in the chapters that follow. The writers offer accounts of how they and others have been able to carve out space to develop relationships, engage in conversation and build communities with young people. Our task is to ensure that what thrives is worthy of doing so and what lost will not be missed. This book is an invitation to explore the contribution that youth work can make towards building happier and more fulfilling lives and communities.

2 | Relationships, friendship and youth work

Huw Blacker

> *A central task for any youth worker has always been the need to construct and sustain educational and social relationships with young people. The nature of these relationships and the ways in which workers need to draw boundaries around them has long been a focus for discussion. In this chapter Huw Blacker explores the place of relationships in youth work, how they can be developed and sustained, the linkages between professional relationships and friendship and the ways in which workers balance authority, friendship and accessibility.*

Relationships are the fabric of our existence, ranging from brief encounters to lifetime commitments. Our thoughts, behaviour, likes and dislikes have all been shaped by relationships past and present. How we spend our time, our 'quality of life', are all impacted by the people we know. Stringer comments that

> The type, nature and quality of relationships in any social setting will have direct impacts on the quality of people's experience, and through that, the quality of outcomes of any human enterprise.
>
> (1999: 29)

In their classic youth work text, Goetschius and Tash (1967: 137) define a relationship as '...a connection between two people in which some sort of exchange takes place'. We may associate these exchanges with 'face-to-face' encounters involving verbal and/or non-verbal communication. We also need to consider, especially given the accessibility of modern technologies such as the Internet and texting, other means by which exchanges occur. For it is via these exchanges that we impact upon one another. Throughout our lives, who we are is being shaped by our own experiences of the actions, opinions and thoughts of others; and by experiencing ourselves and our own actions, opinions and thoughts as others experience and respond towards them.

Our relationships are greatly influenced by our personal circumstances, and by the society in which we live. As children we have relationships with our carers or parents. We attend schools where we relate to peers and teachers. We may pursue leisure interests and belong to youth organisations, sports clubs, orchestras and political parties. We access a variety of 'services' which bring us into contact with people – buying goods from our local shop, taking our car to the garage or visiting our General Practitioner (GP). Institutions generate various social and legal positions that affect how people relate towards each other. We can become employed, unemployed and volunteers. We may be married. We may be adopted. We may be imprisoned.

Through our interactions we learn about various 'ideologies' regarding the relationships we engage in, and how we should conduct ourselves within them.

> Consider how many times someone has given you advice about the sorts of ways to carry on with your relationships . . . they are the places where an ideology about relationships is put into effect, the place where cultural stereotypes of relating are enacted in everyday life.
>
> (Duck 1998: 3)

These 'cultural stereotypes' are also portrayed through the media – watching how people relate in soap operas and sitcoms, magazine articles – all of which contribute to our understanding of relationships. However, our ideas about relationships, and the circumstances in which they develop, are not universally shared. It is easy to overlook this, for 'we are so fully soaked in our own culture that we assume it is normal and we take it for granted' (*op. cit.*: 2). Yet the ideas prevalent in today's society do differ from those of the past, and will change in the future. They are dissimilar from those prevailing in other countries and cultures. Frequently my ideas are different from yours.

On this note I now present to you a collection of such ideas that I have organised into two sections. In the first section I outline a number of themes that help highlight some of the dynamics that come into play and impact our effectiveness in building appropriate and valuable working relationships. In the second section I turn my attention to the concept of friendship and explore this theme in relation to the field of youth work.

Relationships and youth work

Our ability to build and sustain appropriate, effective and valuable relationships with young people is at the heart of youth work practice. How we relate to those we work with and the content of those relationships is our fundamental concern.

The relationships we develop are significantly affected by the circumstances in which they take place and by the knowledge, skills and attitudes brought to these circumstances by those that are relating to each other. In thinking about our working relationships it is important to be aware of, and to think about, the various factors that may impact and influence them. Outlined below are a number of ideas that begin to highlight some of the issues and dynamics we should be considering in our endeavours to build relationships with young people.

What is the purpose of the relationship?

Relationships are influenced to a great extent by their purpose and the expectations we have concerning certain roles in society. If I am in the role of manager, then I will relate to the person I manage in a different way than I would if they were managing me. Both people in the relationship will have certain expectations of the other as to how they may behave. If I visited my GP, I would expect some form of medical advice or treatment. As a student, I would expect my tutor to support my learning. In such functional relationships, it is easy to identify a specific purpose and hence roles are more clearly defined. Yet, there are relationships where boundaries are blurred and the reasons for their being so are frequently complex, for example, those between neighbours or friends.

When considering the relationships between youth workers and young people, the roles are not easily defined. Youth workers are employed, or volunteer, to do a certain job or to take on a specific role. As we have expectations regarding other professionals and the services they offer so too are there expectations as to what we should and should not be doing as professional youth workers. If we are to build relationships that are appropriate to this role, then we need to develop our own sense of purpose. It is important, therefore, that we explore and understand the ideas, principles and expectations underpinning the role of youth worker. It is equally important we explore these ideas critically, recognising them as the 'ideologies' or 'cultural stereotypes' of the present day which have been different in the past and will change in the future.

Youth work practice is framed by a 'knowledge-base' that we must familiarise ourselves with. As we explore this knowledge base through study, practice, supervision, talking with and observing others, so we formulate our own ideas and skills that contribute to how we relate with people in our role as youth worker. For example, central to youth work practice and informal education is the idea of the worker engaging with people in ways that help to promote learning. Tiffany writes:

> Whenever we communicate, we need to be 'on the case': concentrating on identifying, and responding to as many opportunities for promoting learning as possible.
>
> (2001: 96)

Taking on this principle, I would then attempt to put it into practice in my working relationships. I may look for opportunities in everyday conversations to give information or to enter into a debate and pose questions that may lead to reflection on particular topics or experiences. I might organise an activity that is aimed at improving team skills. I may encourage a person I work with to organise an activity themselves, an experience from which they may learn various skills.

As I work at putting this principle into practice, I may learn about and refine my approach further. I might find that if I take this principle into 'overdrive', acting on every opportunity for promoting learning, the relationship itself suffers as people may not want this from me. I might ask myself questions about equality as I may learn from the people I work with just as they may learn from me. I might experience issues around putting this principle into practice covertly or overtly. Through taking on this principle, and attempting to put it into practice, the way in which I perform and hence relate towards young people in my role is significantly affected.

If we enter into relationships with an agenda, then we have a responsibility to communicate this openly. A young person may not be aware of our position, authority or aims in the relationship they have with us. They may have very different expectations or ideas about who you are, what you are doing and the nature of the relationship that they have with you:

> People you work with need to understand who employs you and for what purpose if they are to understand any notion of contract ... There is often no clear contract unless you as a worker negotiate it.
>
> (Tyler 2001: 76)

We may have the opportunity to work in schools, prisons or as detached workers and forget that the people we meet in these environments may have little idea of our role. We may need to clarify concerns such as whether you are in collaboration with teachers, prison officers or the police, as well as explain the service you are there to offer.

Maintaining boundaries

As well as understanding and practising ideas and principles fundamental to the youth work role, we must pay attention to maintaining appropriate boundaries. As professional workers, we need to explore the notion of a 'code of conduct' and be aware of the expectations of what we should *not* be doing in our role. Most organisations have a largely unread 'code of conduct'. For example, the way we should or should not touch a person may not be specifically outlined in a document; we will, however, be expected to act appropriately in relation to this. Again, much of this relates to the cultural ideas prevalent in the context that we work within. It is, therefore, important to explore our own individual values in relation to the ideas and values of others with regard to what we should and should not allow within relationships. There are many areas of debate here in which workers may draw different boundaries (within acceptable parameters of the employing organisation), depending upon their own values and understanding. For example, some may give out their personal phone numbers and take calls outside their working hours, while others may not; when working with young adults some may feel on occasions it is acceptable to accompany them to the pub, whereas others may not.

Context

The environment we operate in affects the possibilities for building and sustaining relationships: are there spaces and opportunities to meet others? When we do meet, are there resources we can use, such as sports equipment, games, computers and music equipment? What can we do together? If we are working in a club or hostel, what are the rules and policies to abide by, enforce or challenge? If we are detached youth workers, do we meet young people in residential areas, shopping areas or in the park? How do these different environments affect the work that we do, and the issues that we have to address?

The hostel where I used to work had a café area, with a television and pool table, where people meet and socialise. Residents shared the same entrance, reception area and lifts into the hostel, increasing the possibilities of meeting other people. As well as the hostel the organisation had other facilities providing activities such as sports and fitness, childcare and youth programmes for people living in the local area. The social spaces used by residents were shared with people attending these activities, as well as the staff facilitating them. These circumstances affect people's tolerance levels towards certain behaviour, such as swearing in front of children, often resulting in a hostel worker being asked to 'have a word' with a resident who may be judged by some as acting inappropriately in this context.

As workers, we must comply with the policies, principles and procedures of the employing agency, which can have a significant impact on our relationships. For example, while working in a hostel I must comply with the agency's drug policies, which state that if a resident brings illegal drugs onto the premises, they may be evicted from their accommodation. Consequently, a resident may feel uncomfortable about discussing their drug use, knowing they risk losing their home if they tell me anything which details that they are using drugs on the premises. This creates a dilemma for me: I see it as within the remit of my role to work with people around drug issues, but taking on the position of hostel worker I also have a duty to operate within a given legal framework. This issue had serious consequences some years ago for two workers based in a hostel for the homeless in Cambridge who were jailed for allowing drugs to be exchanged on their premises without reporting those involved to the police (Burrell 2000; McKeown 2006). The agency they worked for operated a policy of confidentiality which was widely accepted at the time, under which information about residents would not generally be disclosed to outside agencies, including the police. The case raised a number of issues for concern among other similar organisations affecting the work they were able, or willing, to undertake in the light of these legal implications. Some agencies chose not to accommodate drug addicts and others experienced staff shortages as workers did not want to risk imprisonment for failure to inform on those they worked with. The hostel in which I worked continues to experience the repercussions of this case as their drug policy, developed in response to the Cambridge incident, reflected such concerns and hence impacts upon the information workers can legally share in their relationships with residents.

Our context frames the ideas people may have about the role we perform. A youth worker in a hostel will be perceived differently to one based in a drugs project, with different expectations about the services we offer. Taking on explicit roles in specific contexts immediately affects the content people will share with us in our relationships.

Communication

As youth workers we also need to consider the effectiveness of our communication skills. Duck contends that we use talk as a vehicle for creating change in relationships, for handling conflict and for displaying various emotions and attitudes. We express our personalities and talk about our desires and goals. We resolve disputes, forgive, complain, get out of relationships and deal with enemies; in short, we talk to relate, whether well or badly (Duck 1998: 7). As workers, we need to be thoughtful about this process. Are we communicating well or badly? Are we using language that can be understood? What are we trying to communicate and why? What do we choose not to say and why? Similarly, we need to think about non-verbal communication and how our 'body language' can affect our interactions. If, for example, a person is talking to me and I keep looking at my watch, then they may perceive this as a signal that I want them to stop, that I am disinterested or that I have something more important to do. Sometimes this may be appropriate, other times not (see the various contributions to Robb *et al.* 2004).

Much of our everyday conversation is based around taken-for-granted responses – clichés and patterns we use throughout the day, such as asking 'How are you?', to which a high percentage of the time we receive a response similar to 'Fine, thank you'. As workers, it is useful to see conversation as more of an adventure that can transcend the banal. I have worked, for example, in settings where there are a significant number of unemployed people. It is common to hear talk of boredom and of the lack of money to do anything. Conversations can add to or reinforce this sense of boredom, or they can be a means by which this boredom is transcended.

Communication is also about silence and listening. Allowing someone the space to tell their story is of great importance. A person may not be seeking our judgement or opinion on what they say, but they may simply seek the opportunity to relate it and to share their life with someone.

Doing things together

Sometimes we have the opportunity and the resources to vary the context in which we work. For example, the role of the hostel worker involves a responsibility to organise, or to encourage residents to organise, various activities. These range from activities such as bowling, pool tournaments, craft nights, cinema trips and karaoke to a weekly 'outdoor adventure' session, a DJ project and cooking sessions. We also organise regular trips away for several days or weekends. It is recognised that these activities have a substantial impact on the relationships between staff and residents and between residents themselves. A new resident can quickly get to know others by attending an activity. People have more opportunity to develop their social networks, as well as learn from each other and from the activity. When staff go away with residents for a few days the relationship often develops and grows dramatically. The experience of being away from the hostel without having to enforce certain rules and policies allows a different dynamic to surface. The role of the hostel worker has acquired a different connotation in these circumstances. The opportunity to get to know one another, to have more time to talk (often late into the night), to have a 'task' that we need to work on together or to take part in an activity we would not often have the chance to do contribute to the building of the relationship. As Darling *et al.* note, somewhat ironically, relationships are often best built 'when building a relationship was *not* the main purpose for getting together' (1994: 228).

As a hostel worker, there are also many other day-to-day opportunities for 'doing things together' – filling in a Housing Benefit form with a resident, having a coffee, playing pool, going to court, eating dinner together or watching television. All contribute to the process of relationships being built. For many workers these opportunities are more limited. This may be due to lack of funding, resources or the format of the environment in which they work. In these circumstances, 'doing things together' may require more effort and creativity on the part of the worker. Even the simplest of ideas can be highly effective. As a detached youth worker I remember attempting to build relationships with a group of young men from a council estate. After meeting a couple of times and establishing who we were my colleague and I were experiencing a sense of awkwardness each time we met with the group, who would make their excuses and leave after talking with us for 5 to 10 minutes. We then decided to take a football with us. Arriving on the estate my colleague and I kicked the ball back and forth as we approached the group, who immediately joined in a spontaneous kick about. We suggested playing a 'proper game' over the park and proceeded to play for over an hour together.

During the game we had the opportunity to make positive comments about the football skills of players, even if they were not very good (e.g., 'good pass'/'well played'/'good tackle'). We experienced the comradeship of passing the ball to each other, learning their names and shouting them out as they had a reason to shout out our names, setting up shots on goal and giving 'high fives' when we scored; we proposed changing the teams after half an hour so we could play on the same side as other group members. Following this session our relationships changed dramatically. As we left, we were asked when we would be coming back again. When we did go back 2 days later, we were greeted with enthusiasm. The sense of awkwardness had gone as members of the group seemed happy to sit and chat with us for a couple of hours. An activity, as so often is the case in youth work, had helped to erode barriers and encourage the building of relationships thereby opening up routes to learning.

Personality

Although we may each refer to similar ideas and principles in our attempt to understand our role, we interpret and implement such ideas in varying ways. We have our own individual differences; hence the way in which we work will in some respect vary from others. As we bring our own experiences to bear on our practice, we are likely to give prominence to certain values and beliefs while questioning others. Although there is a core of knowledge, skills and attitudes considered essential to good youth work, all effective workers develop their own distinctive professional identity around these. 'Text book theories' can inform and guide our practice, but it is our unique way of engaging with people that breathes life into our work. Here, it is important to consider our own personality and the impact this has upon our relationships. We need to think about who we are, what qualities we bring to our interactions and how our personality affects our relationships. Palmer helpfully highlights the importance of self-awareness/self-evaluation:

> Teaching, like any truly human activity, emerges from one's inwardness, for better or worse. As I teach, I project the condition of my soul onto my students, my subject, and our way of being together ... teaching holds a mirror to the soul. If I am willing to look in that mirror and not run from what I see, I have a chance to gain self-knowledge – and knowing myself is as crucial to good teaching as knowing my students and my subject.
>
> (1998: 2)

As relationships are central to our practice, 'knowing ourselves' is of fundamental importance if we are to understand why we relate to some people better than others. We have a responsibility to look at ourselves rather than, for example, explaining a 'relationship breakdown' entirely as caused by the personality traits of the other person. We also need to consider how we can maintain relationships with people we may not like or who may not like us. To dislike each other does not mean you cannot develop an effective relationship. We are employed, like other welfare workers such as social workers, medics and teachers, to work alongside people, irrespective of our likes and dislikes towards them. For me, the ability to develop relationships here raises a number of points: I have a responsibility of providing an appropriate service to those I am employed to serve; importantly, am I able to recognise and 'hold' any dislikes I may experience and reflect on the reasons for my dislike, that is, are they born of my own prejudice? Do I understand why I may dislike someone? Am I making biased decisions/judgements or acting inappropriately because of the influence of my dislike? Am I being true to myself? Can I use my sense of dislike constructively in the way that I work? If appropriate, can I explore my dislike for someone with them, or explore their dislike of me – if handled carefully learning can come from this and mutual ground may be discovered.

Positioning

Much of the effectiveness of our work depends on how we 'pitch' our approach, and how we view ourselves in relation to others, that is, our 'positioning'. We can engage with those we work with in a number of ways. If, for instance, I was to deal with the issue of a young person's rent arrears while living in the hostel, I could tell them what to do (Authoritarian – 'Pay your rent or you will be evicted'); or present them with the problem and devise some solutions together (Negotiation – 'You're in rent arrears, what do you suggest you and I do about it?'). These two different approaches can create very different dynamics in the relationship and lead to very dissimilar outcomes. Asking the resident what they are going to do places the responsibility in their hands; this approach is more akin to 'client self-determination'.

We could also consider the concept of positioning in relation to a council estate that may have a lack of useful facilities for young people. Is this recognised as an issue worth addressing, or is the behaviour of the young person, who may be responding to these circumstances, the only focus of attention? We can see how the current 'position' of the government towards this issue can greatly affect outcomes and ultimately people's lives. More powers are being given to the police to enforce curfews or to exclude people from certain areas. The focus seems to be more on the behaviour of the young person rather than on possible root causes of their behaviour (Waiton 2008).

A question that often arises for youth workers regarding their positioning is how this relates to the concept of 'friendship'. The relationships we develop in youth work are primarily on an informal, voluntary basis. Those we work with do not have to relate with us if they choose not to. This re-emphasises the importance of our personality, the 'positioning' we take and the qualities we bring to our work. For a voluntary relationship to develop, characteristics such as trust, talking and listening, doing things together, acceptance, respect and building rapport are important, as is showing care and upholding obligations towards each other (see

Smith and Smith 2008). A special kind of relationship develops, but is this entering the domain of friendship and if so is this appropriate? This brings me to the second section of this chapter, in which I turn my attention to the theme of friendship.

Friendship

What is 'friendship'?

Friendship is a difficult social phenomenon to define as the term is used to cover a variety of informal relationships. Sherman suggests that 'a friendship is relational, something between rather than in a person' (1997: 188). What, then, takes place *between* people that may lead to the term 'friend' being used?

In *Being Friends*, Levin (1987) lists some 'ingredients' that are characteristics of a friendship:

Friends CARE and CHERISH	Friends TRUST one another
Friends GIVE and RECEIVE	Friends TALK and LISTEN and CONFIDE in each other
Friends DO THINGS TOGETHER	Friends are ATTRACTED to each other
Friends have RAPPORT	Friends REACH OUT to each other
Friends ACCEPT and RESPECT	Friends take on OBLIGATIONS

While this list provides a number of relational characteristics that may be useful to contemplate, it is not a comprehensive checklist. Such lists highlight the difficulties we face with language. We use terms such as 'close' and 'best' friend, with each meaning different things to different people in various contexts, for we may 'care' in different ways, and have discrete meanings for 'trust' and 'rapport'. Friendship, and the language we use when discussing it, can be ambiguous. Aristotle (in Sherman 1997) explores the notion of friendship by presenting three different classifications:

- Friends that are based on UTILITY;
- Friends based on PLEASURE;
- Friends based on VIRTUE, or CHARACTER FRIENDSHIPS.

He describes friendships of utility as being transient and likened to the word utility itself, that is, the condition of being useful or profitable. This relates to friends that help us in ways such as the lending of a lawnmower or studying together. Friends based on pleasure are more like the people you meet in pubs and go to the gym with once a week or share an interest, such as music, with. Finally, Aristotle describes friends of virtue as spending more time together and becoming familiar with each other's characters. They are individuals who share sentiments such as trust, good will and mutual concern towards each other. Such a friendship does not develop instantly but materialises over time.

We also need to consider how gender differences may impact the friendships between people. As each society has ideas about how we should conduct our relationships, so too are there ideas relating to gender roles and how girls and boys, men and women are 'expected' to behave. Various gender stereotypes affect the way people then relate to one another, for example, 'men don't cry'.

friendship and context

As with relationships, the nature of friendships and the opportunities for them to develop are affected by circumstance. The hostel I have talked about provides accommodation for young adults, many of whom are leaving home and living 'independently' for the first time. These circumstances influence the nature of the relationships they develop. For as Pahl explains, for them, like so many others in different circumstances, 'friends may be taking over various social tasks, duties and functions from family and kin, simply out of practical necessity' (2000: 8).

As our circumstances change, so do the relationships and friendships we engage in and the qualities which we draw from them. Again, to quote Pahl, 'friends can be described as having different degrees of importance and significance . . . at different stages of their lives' (ibid.: 9). We may choose to live with a partner, get married or start a family; our employment and economic circumstances may change. These can affect the significance of our friends, for example, our partner may take over certain 'social tasks, duties and functions' that we previously sought from friends. However, we may then turn to friends for other support needs, such as babysitting.

While we may gain various benefits, material and emotional, from friendship, it is important to recognise friendship as being valuable in its own right:

> A friend is not for use or help . . . for when we need nothing, we still seek others to share our enjoyment . . . . It would still be valued as an intrinsic good and we would still choose it even if nothing further resulted from it . . . It adds

something in it's own right to happiness, and the absence of it takes something away.

(Sherman 1997: 209)

Youth workers as friends?

Friendship is a concept that, historically and presently, holds an importance at the core of youth work. The notion of the worker 'befriending' young people is a term that is often used by youth workers, though not all would agree that to be friends with those we are employed to work with is an appropriate way of thinking about our work. However, as youth work has become more *professionalised* so those we work with have become more frequently referred to as 'clients', and greater attention paid to maintaining 'appropriate boundaries' in our 'professional relationships' (Collander-Brown in this book). As this change has occurred so the concept of 'worker as friend' has become increasingly marginalised. While it is viewed as acceptable to be friendly in our working relationships, there is more controversy around the notion of 'being a friend'. Yet, within some arenas of 'people work', this notion has prevailed:

> Within youth work there has been a parallel interest in friends as educators. It has similarly taken two forms: conceptualizing the youth worker or leader as a friend to young people; and looking to the role of peers as teachers. While the former has tended to become rather unfashionable within professionalized youth agencies, it still has a strong presence within social movement work – and particularly practice linked to churches.

(Doyle and Smith 2002)

When reflecting on my own practice, I can refer to Aristotle's three different classifications of friendship and compare how my actions relate to these concepts: I give hostel residents lifts to the train station (friends of utility). I regularly go climbing and kayaking with groups of residents (friends of pleasure). I have spent many months getting to know some residents, with sentiments developing between us such as trust and mutual concern, good will, sharing and confiding (friends of virtue). While I may be carrying out these actions, I also have to recognise that I am being paid to be in these relationships. If we hold that 'friendship is ideally founded on sentiments, not rights or duties' (Bell and Coleman 1999: 9), then I have to question my motivations regarding the above actions, and the implications this has for understanding such relationships. However, while I am employed to be in these relationships with a duty to perform, I also experience sentiments that occasionally develop between myself and some residents that can be seen to be in the domain of friendship. 'Being paid' does not necessarily get in the way of various qualities developing within the working relationship. As Doyle and Smith wrote:

> The informal and personal relationships involved have some element of choice… There can come a point where payment is really a side issue – it is the shared pursuit of the good that matters.
>
> (2002)

While sentiments akin to friendship may develop in the relationships I form with certain individuals, I still need to maintain appropriateness in these relationships with regard to the role I am in. I need to think carefully about boundaries and pay attention to the implication of my actions and judgements being affected by 'favouritism'. I also need to question whether I am prioritising my own needs, for example, to be liked and appreciated. Essentially, while certain qualities may develop in the relationships I have with those I work with I must not allow these to get in the way of acting professionally. Often the relationships I develop with people who can understand, appreciate and respect the boundaries that should be held are the ones that are more likely to develop into friendships.

Much of the debate surrounding friendship and youth work centres around the use of language and the ambiguous nature of 'umbrella terms' such as 'friendship'. Just as some societies have many words to describe different aspects of love (love of parent, love of friend or love of partner), maybe what our language and thinking is lacking is a similar depth of appreciation towards different aspects of friendship.

Young people, friendship and learning

In the hostel that has been the focus of my attention there are up to 150 residents living in the same building. Residents often consulted me when they experienced relationship problems while living in this environment. My role often entailed an element of 'teaching' about relationships and friendship with people, and exploring with them why they may be experiencing difficulties. My effectiveness and ability to do this was impacted by how well I know the person I am working with. I may have had the opportunity to see how a person interacts and relates towards people over a period of time, as they may live in the hostel for several months. Alongside this I may have had experience of that person and the way they have related towards me. From this I may well be in a position to reflect back to this person some of my own thoughts regarding the way they present themselves to other people. Aristotle says that:

friends supply us with the mirror that we lack on our own. As such, they figure crucially in our projects of self-knowledge ... we have a moral duty ... to be honest with friends about their faults and weaknesses, and to offer such criticisms without intent to harm.

(quoted in Sherman 1997: 233)

In my role as hostel worker, I often attempted to create opportunities in which new residents moving into the hostel can meet others and develop friendships. As one resident told me:

I didn't know anybody when I moved in. It came to the stage when I was sitting around all day on my own in my little room, with just a radio. It was getting ridiculous. I had no social life. It was a very lonely place to be. (Interview)

Residents who are 'friendless' may often turn to workers for companionship. In doing so, the worker may then engage with this person in ways that can address building and sustaining relationships with others. This could be through simply introducing them to others or inviting them to take part in a group activity. It could also entail conversations about relating to people and discussing difficulties a person may be experiencing in this respect, while together exploring possible ways of overcoming these. Relationships hold a wealth of benefits. Putnam (2000), when researching the notion of 'social capital', explores the possible impact of well-developed social networks (the social connections we have with others) on people's lives. His claims include that 'social networks foster norms of reciprocity that encourage attention to others welfare' (p. 117); that '... civic connections help make us healthy, wealthy and wise' (p. 287); that 'social networks provide people with advice, job leads, strategic information ...' (p. 319); and that 'The more integrated we are with our community, the less likely we are to experience colds, heart attacks, strokes, cancer, depression, and premature death of all sorts' (p. 326).

Friendships can help to facilitate activity in our lives. I have friends I go kayaking with, play guitar with, meet in the pub and go on holidays with. As I engage in these activities, I have the opportunity to learn new skills and to learn about myself in different circumstances. The more we open ourselves up to others, the more we can learn and grow as people. As we confide in others, we actually take the time to reflect on our own lives. The same applies to our work. If we are less guarded and not clinging to our position of authority but meet others and let them meet us as people in our own right, then we are likely to be challenged and inspired by them.

In conclusion

To return to my starting point, relationships lie at the heart of our existence and inevitably meaningful, productive relationships provide the essential ingredient of all successful youth work encounters. Yet herein lies a profound difficulty. They are the vital ingredient yet are impossible to realistically measure in terms of effectiveness and outcomes (Smith and Smith 2008: 108–111). How can workers score and gauge the effect we may be having on others, let alone calculate the value that someone else chooses to place on their relationship with us? Yet although relationships rarely feature in terms of measured outcomes with regards to our work, it is worth remembering just how important a relationship may be in its own right. We can appeal to the research literature and be sure that close relationships are central to well-being (Vangelisti and Perlman 2006). Even if we do not consciously 'educate' or 'counsel' but spend our time 'being' with someone, then we may be doing something of incalculable value.

3 | Engaging in conversation

Heather Smith

> *Youth workers are constantly engaged in conversations with young people, colleagues and members of the wider community. An ability to use words with sensitivity and skill is an essential attribute for all youth workers. Heather Smith looks at ways in which we can foster productive conversations and use them in our practice.*

Conversation is a necessary and central feature of life. It enables us to get through each day by helping to secure the things we want, need and desire. However, from an early age, we begin to see that it is not just about getting things done; it is a way of communicating with humanity, creating a feeling of being connected to others. Without it individuals can feel isolated and cut off. Conversation is, therefore, much more than a tool; it is an art that takes time and care to craft (Blyth 2008).

Conversation can encourage and sustain the articulation of ideas and emotions. However, to do this we need a broad vocabulary. We also need to understand language – the ways in which words are employed to convey meaning. Sometimes, though, words fail us. We may have a sense that the words we are using are inadequate to the task of expressing what we believe or feel. For some of us this may lead to frustration and anger and this may show in our behaviour. Others may become distant and disengage. At such times we need the ability to look beyond the words being used and explore ideas such as persona, expression, intonation and the space between the words. We also need to attend to our feelings. These are things we will look at further into the chapter.

Ways of talking

There is within conversation a degree of natural order, which may involve observing the need for pleasantries, idle chit-chat and silence. The ability to follow this order projects your persona as socially acceptable and non-forceful. It will often lay the foundation for further encounters. People tend to avoid those who make them feel uncomfortable and do not pay due regard to social conventions. However, for youth workers it is not always an option to do this. As the previous chapter stressed, youth workers are constantly required to work with those who they may not like or who act in ways of which they disapprove. We are, in many cases, employed to work with and alongside individuals and groups who are either unaware of or determined to reject such conventions. As youth workers we have to learn, and be committed to, the different ways of engaging in conversation with those who others may feel uncomfortable talking to. Conversation lies at the heart of informal education and youth work. It is the dominant mode of working. All else is peripheral.

Although conversation is largely a spoken means of communication, it cannot exist in a vacuum. It is multi-dimensional not only in methods and uses, but also in context and meaning. Throughout this chapter reference will be made to different types of talk. In order to work through and around this topic it is helpful to begin by making two simple distinctions:

Chit-chat and banter – Talk involving, for example, pleasantries, comments that pass the time of day, verbal sparring and the exchange of information. This may require skill but this is talk that does not necessarily involve deep attention to others and significant reflection.

Conversation and dialogue – Two-way talk, discussion of mutually selected topics that can involve the disclosure of emotions, opinions and feelings, and offer a more complex and in-depth discussion of topics.

Some will dispute this division, arguing, for example, that chit-chat and banter are forms of conversation (Wardhaugh 1985). The separation here relates to the way many workers talk about their activities. We might hear a worker saying, for example, 'Nothing much happened tonight we just had a natter.' It is essential for youth workers to be able to engage in these forms of talk. Self-evidently, according to this definition, the second category is of a higher order than the first although we must never underestimate the importance of chit-chat and banter within the context of our work. They oil the wheels of relationships. Generally they are the first point of contact or of renewal. Few young people meet us for the first time and engage in dialogue. They test us out and make judgements about us on the basis of how we respond. They look to see whether we listen to what they say, or whether we can respond to their jokes and pleasantries. Sullen and distant workers are unlikely to be able to make the leap into deeper forms of conversation.

When discussing our practice as youth workers we sometimes use the term dialogue to describe exchanges we have had with young people. Clearly at times the words conversation and dialogue are used interchangeably. On other occasions workers refer to an encounter as being a 'dialogue' to convey that what had occurred was deeper and more substantive than mere conversation. When this happens we meet a long-standing debate regarding the relationship between 'dialogue' and 'conversation'. For some philosophers, theologians and educationalists a clear divide exists between the two. Indeed, the unique characteristics of dialogue are such that they may, like Buber (2002), endeavour to isolate discrete forms. Certainly youth work, at its best, is an inheritor of an educational tradition stretching back over 2500 years of recorded history based on the Socratic dialogue, viewing education as a process of talk and exchange designed to draw forth knowledge and understanding. The division between dialogue and conversation within the context of youth work may, however, be unhelpful. It devalues conversation without specifying what the unique features of each are. Then, we must ask ourselves, when does a conversation transform itself into a dialogue, or a dialogue 'degenerate' into conversation? In the context of practice are they not intrinsically linked? Indeed workers allow, perhaps even encourage, chit-chat to deepen and move forward. Youth workers operate on a sliding-scale that takes them from the superficial conversation or chit-chat to the profound and life-changing. The former is commonplace, the later rare. Handling both, we must acknowledge, requires expertise and sensitivity. Therapists may be uncomfortable with the former, school teachers with the latter. Youth workers, because they work in the realm of the informal rather than in the office or classroom, must be prepared to handle both and all conversational points in-between (Smith and Smith 2008: 93–112).

Wardhaugh (1985) helps us to understand the complexity of conversation, its social norms and uses, and offers a means of better relating this activity to practice. Besides identifying the degree to which conversation is a co-operative undertaking and a public activity, he draws our attention to some of the skills that 'successful' conversationalists employ. These are summarised as follows:

- A well-developed feeling of what we can or cannot say;
- Knowing how to use words and what words we can use in different circumstances;

- An ability to supplement and reinforce what we say with appropriate behaviour;
- An ability to attune ourselves to how others employ the same skills (Wardhaugh 1985: 4).

Conversation is far more intricate than a set of words or sentences. Some of the skills that are identified above are not inherited; they are learnt by being in a variety of social and professional settings alongside a wide range of different people. Conversation cannot be learnt from a textbook. It is an art acquired by being with people. Via interaction and observation we learn and understand how others work and this will then both inform and aid how we relate to people.

Trusting in conversation

Our intent in a conversation is open to interpretation by others, as is theirs by us. Because of this, trust will play an important part in any conversation that occurs (Jeffs and Smith 2005: 30). This is not necessarily specific to a relationship but is more a generalised trust in human nature. It embodies an assumption that most people we encounter will not set out to intentionally hurt or damage us. Such trust enables us to assume people will conduct themselves in appropriate ways with few seeking to cause a scene or draw undue attention to themselves. This adherence to social rules leads individuals to avoid confrontation or challenging any inappropriateness in the way they are spoken to by others. Equally, we assume that the other has adequate skills to sustain the conversation (Wardhaugh 1985: 10). But what if an individual lacks such skills and understanding? The ability to work with this and, perhaps, to challenge the way in which others interact with us is an important task.

For a time I worked with young men who had significant emotional and behavioural difficulties. The environment was difficult, yet it called for a nurturing way of being and a relentless acceptance of the negativity thrown at you each day, in the forms of verbal, mental and physical abuse. Each young man displayed varying signs of being unable to deal with the world adequately, and an inability to communicate on a level that truly articulated the way they felt. This was often manifested through violence towards property or people, or disengagement with the world around them. Their vocabulary was often limited and their understanding of the theory of language low. Through gentle yet straightforward confrontation within conversation, I was able to challenge their way of communication. It was often difficult and required a huge amount of commitment on my part to be consistent and willingness to confront the same things repeatedly. Challenges would be mounted over the use of certain words, name calling and attitude. This went alongside gentle prompting and encouraging them to find ways of expressing feelings appropriately. Asking a young man to re-articulate how he feels without swearing or being aggressive requires us to be firm yet non-threatening, patient and above all to not rely on our supposed authority as an adult or worker. Challenge here is not about us gaining control of the situation or being comfortable with the feelings being expressed and words used. Rather it is concerned with understanding and caring about how someone may relate to another in the realms of the wider social context. Challenge for challenge's sake is not helpful and can often be counter-productive. In more specific terms, confrontation in order to humiliate, show someone up or impose our assumed authority simply shows our own lack of ability to communicate and deal adequately with a given situation. The ability to communicate and engage in conversation with such young people is not something most people acquire within the normal course of their lives. Rather it is a skill or art that workers must consciously seek to learn and polish, and to develop over time.

Forms of talk

Wardhaugh suggests each conversation is like a small piece of theatre, and within it we acquire a role. The role we have within any given encounter may determine the type of talk we engage in, its content and its purpose. There are times when an individual is put in the role of a confidante or sounding board and quite often this is part of a growing friendship. People use each other to discuss problems or ideas, and share what is going on in their lives. This enables them to feel connected to each other. However, when an individual has this role forced upon them, then it can sometimes become a one-way encounter. Unless attention is paid to balance and mutuality an individual may become labelled as self-absorbed and unaware of the social skills needed to engage in talk with another. Generally people become skilled at avoiding entering into conversation with such individuals. In contrast, when someone comes to us within our professional setting, the encounter may be specific and focused on the other. They may omit chit-chat and enter straightaway into a serious conversation about themselves and their experiences. For workers this may be deemed acceptable, even desirable, because the setting and purpose and our role shape the encounter.

It is important to acknowledge and appreciate the value of the different forms of talking. Whichever form of talk-type makes an individual feel connected at any one point depends very much on their emotional state at the time. Forcing conversational encounters, or demanding they be of one type, may do more harm than good. Light-hearted banter might not be appropriate at a funeral, but fine a few hours later. With so many different ways of talking how do we move between them in the short pockets of time we have with one another? In all settings, both professional and personal, chit-chat and banter is often a precursor to any deeper conversation. Talk about 'trivia' can be the key to establishing safe ground between two people. It can begin to foster trust and the natural order within conversation. People often avoid disclosure until they feel safe. There needs to be a commitment to working with uncertainty regarding both time and subject matter. Although many of us would like to get to the bottom of issues quickly, this is usually not possible. It is often a willingness to allow people to talk that enables them to identify their own solutions.

The place of self

It is important to consider that somewhere along the line, within a worker–young person relationship, we will be asked questions about ourselves. This is a fine line to tread because it is important the focus doesn't shift, and the encounters become about us. However, it needs to be appreciated that people will not often share information with a stranger, although there are circumstances, for example, in counselling relationships where this occurs. Generally, people need to have a sense of who you are before they discuss anything personal with you. This is where conversation skills enable us to deflect questions that might be too personal and could compromise our working relationship. At the same time we need to provide enough information to satisfy the other person's need to know something about us.

Workers can have real problems around consistency because of the voluntary nature of the youth work encounter, the range of settings it takes place in and the limitless number of topics that may arise in conversation. If we wish to develop our relationships with people and progress through to deeper levels of conversation, we must take care to present a consistent persona but at the same time be real. Without it we may create an underlying feeling of mistrust or distance. This is something Carl Rogers discusses, and encapsulates by remarking that 'being trustworthy does not demand that I be rigidly consistent but that I be dependably real' (2001: 119). Authenticity is the key. Being oneself is essential, if we are to avoid being caught out as 'dishonest'; however, that does not mean one can behave in ways inappropriate to the setting. Rather it demands reflection, analysis and understanding of the place and context within which the conversation and dialogue is occurring (see Smith and Smith 2008: 13–22).

If we are skilled in the art of conversation, we will know when a young person is sounding us out. We listen and wait for key phrases or statements. The 'should I have done that?' or the 'why does x treat me like that?' type questions that can be left hanging in air for the worker to respond to or overlook. These and similar remarks are often easy to detect because they come with no explanation and often appear to be thrown-in in the hope we will catch them. At other times people need issues to be teased out. They may only allow difficult questions and concerns to enter into the conversation or be developed when they are comfortable with us. Such a feeling of acceptance can negate the need for pleasantries – the natural order of conversation can be displaced. But it is only on mutual understanding that this can happen; without it we may rightly be considered rude and our actions socially unacceptable.

Although it is not advisable to force the pace of conversation in normal circumstances, there is a necessity at times to quickly change gear. This is where the ability to attune to another becomes of paramount importance. If you feel that an individual is trying to open up to you and you wish to pursue this, it is essential that the individual, who is disclosing, feels safe, nurtured, cared for and sympathised with. The ability to achieve this marks you out as gifted in conversation. Contextual support of a conversation is crucial. People will know if what you are saying is rehearsed. Your pursuit of dialogue must be spontaneous, and the individual should feel that it is so. This is again something that Rogers picks up on, 'It is also worth noting that is the way in which his (*the therapist*) attitudes and procedures are perceived which makes a difference to the client, and that it is this perception which is crucial' (2001: 113).

Space

The big question is how do you achieve this? There are basic ways to make someone feel comfortable, such as non-confrontational eye contact, affirmative noises, questioning, clarifying and being non-judgemental. However, one of the most important is space. True connection with another happens when space is created to allow it to happen. If people feel you have time for them and there is time to talk, they will take advantage of this opportunity. The creation of space can be achieved through things such as tasks but your being and persona are the keys. Undertaking some task, such as re-stocking the coffee bar, allows people to talk while the focus is on something else. For one thing it takes away the possibility of uncomfortable and invasive eye contact. For example, although washing-up is a mundane task, when two people are side-by-side with no real opportunity for eye contact, it is surprising the depth of conversation that can occur. I have also worked as part of a team who support families with children who have terminal or life-threatening illnesses. We did this by offering the whole family respite in a home-from-home setting. The focus was not on having endless 'meaningful' conversations, but on family time, rest, recuperation and on having a place where the family could simply 'be'. However, as part of my practice I did engage in 'meaningful' conversations, and many of these took place when I was focused on a task. This happened for a variety of reasons. People may have felt that the task required me to be where I was and so they were not taking up my time. The approach was on their terms because I was fixed where I was as long as the task required, yet they could walk away when they needed to. There was also the factor that my full attention was not on them and this can take away the uncomfortable feelings that one-to-one conversations often create. What is essential, and indicative of the environment, was that the type of talk engaged in is up to the family member.

If you are experienced as someone who is calm, accepting, generous, understanding and non-judgemental, you will naturally attract people to you. This is experienced through being rather than words. Your role, be it in a personal or professional relationship, must be experienced as genuine, otherwise you may be seen as mocking it (Goffman 1969: 28). You need to be who you say you are and your actions need to complement your claim. In other words, you need to be authentic. An understanding of human nature is fundamental; the ability to empathise is central, what if that was you in their situation? This comes by being around others and attuning yourself to them. Putting this in words for others to achieve is hard; many of these qualities are part of who you are and the reason you are in the practice you are in. Rogers argues that 'it is the attitudes and feelings of the therapist, rather than his theoretical orientation, which is important. His procedures and techniques are less important than his attitudes' (2001: 113). People talk to people they feel comfortable with, not those who work to a formula.

Conversation and dialogue are process-orientated. Kane (2003: 76) argues that through telling our stories we begin to gain meaning from them, and if they stay within us they can stagnate. By allowing another to tell you their stories, you create an opportunity for them to make sense of their experiences. This is where the need for a focus on process, not goal, becomes apparent. As soon as we try to lead the other person to some outcome, rather than engaging with what is being said and allowing the conversation to lead us, we lose our way. The process is not about finding a solution or placing definitive meanings on people's experiences but rather the individual finding their own meaning. Once you have been able to articulate how you are feeling or an experience you have had, it makes it real and brings it into the public domain. This can often stop things festering because, more often than not, the issue stops growing as the individual begins to understand and deal with it.

Silence is an important factor within the conversational process. Kane, again, identifies the ways that silence can bring focus. Silence does not necessarily mean that someone has stopped engaging in the conversation; rather they may be assembling thoughts that have not been expressed before (2003: 54). All too often people wish to fill the silence, seeing it as awkward and non-productive. If you are a person who engages in different forms of talk regularly, you will know that silences occur fairly frequently, and you will recognise when people begin to feel uncomfortable. As Wardhaugh (1985) identifies, this is because silence signifies to individuals that there is a breakdown in what should be a co-operative undertaking. Parker J. Palmer (1998) also points out that silence is often seen as a symptom that something is going wrong. However, silence is also about space, and productive silence allows an individual to gather their thoughts while they are in the company of another. The feeling of connectedness continues through the silence. As you become more attuned to how others work and express themselves, both generally and specifically within the relationships you have, you become able to discern when the silence is about space and thought collection and when it is about awkwardness. Kane offers us a rule in these circumstances: if what you are going to say is better or worth more than the silence, then break the silence; if it is not, then don't!

It is important not to treat talk as simply an intellectual or professional exercise. Although there may need to be a certain level of professionalism with regard to disclosure and boundaries, there needs to be a level of humanness – which exceeds the professionalism. By separating our own suffering from that of the person we are engaging with, a distancing of emotion is being created. That is not to say that we should allow ourselves to become swept up in the emotion of the situation, but more that we should not separate ourselves from what we are feeling. In order to achieve compassion in what we do there is a need to expand our 'selfhood' to include the other. Kane (2003: 138) talks about this as compassion's technology. Rogers (2001: 120) develops this line of thinking also. He remarks that 'if I am to facilitate the personal growth of others in relation to me, then I must grow, and while this is often painful it is also enriching.'

In conclusion

The aim of this chapter has been to explore the notion of conversation and how we may use this in our practice. We have seen the concept of conversation is so much more than verbal communication. I have purposefully steered away from the logistics of how to have a conversation and focused on how who we are makes a difference to the type of conversations we have and why as individuals we may need to feel connected to another. As workers our attitude and ability to attune ourselves to another is essential. Often in practice the conversations we have are about people's development or issues that they are going through, all of which require sensitivity and compassion. However, using the right words is not enough; we must be accepting of what is being said without seeking to make ourselves comfortable with the words expressed, have the ability to gently challenge and respect the silences that may occur.

In any context there needs to be an appreciation that conversation is not a process of logic. Wardhaugh (1985: 36) sees it as a maze. Within a conversation you have to recheck, backtrack, hypothesise and live with the uncertainty that any type of talk can leave us with. Talking with another is not a logistic exercise, but more an encounter of emotions. There is no formula for how to be successful in conversation. Throughout this chapter this is something that I have consciously reiterated with almost every point. You may understand the social graces and the underpinning theory of how you may relate to another, yet this will not create the type of communication that makes two individuals feel connected. The ability to 'be' with another takes time, and it involves becoming comfortable with silences, accepting uncertainty and that we may not always feel comfortable with what is being expressed.

Talk of any type plays an enormous part in informal education and youth work. In order that it becomes effective within practice, we must be open to it. It is easy to shut someone down and not acknowledge the needs expressed. The difficulties come when we give people the space to tell their stories. It is in this space that the rawness of life is exposed, and individuals must expand their selfhood to include the other. The expansion of selfhood is what makes us feel connected to another even if we do at times leave the encounter feeling less intact than when we began.

4 Being with an other as a professional practitioner: uncovering the nature of working with individuals

David Collander-Brown

> *Youth workers have always predominately fixed their attention upon the group, whether in the club or on the street. The bulk of youth work texts reflect this pre-occupation. However, in all settings workers will at times be required to focus on the individual. In this chapter David Collander-Brown examines how this shift in emphasis can be effectively managed; how youth workers can create the space for the individual within the practice setting.*

In the midst of all the new technical-sounding verbiage concerning targets and outcomes it is easy to lose sight of the truth that it is the relationship between the young person and youth worker that is central to the work. It is our relationship with a young person upon which most of our work, as a practitioner, hinges. And this is a relationship that can '*develop only when the persons involved pay attention to one another*' (Barry and Connolly 1986: 47). What effective workers with individual young people do is highly skilled work, drawing on, through different stages in the process, a range of diverse roles and capacities. Done well the practitioner moves seamlessly through the stages, but the unifying core is the relationship between young person and the worker. Building face-to-face skills cannot be done impersonally. It requires personal exploration and reflection with a trainer or supervisor. The title *being with another* points to the quality of process within this work. It is not a *task-centred* way of working. The *uncovering* is not a final description of method, but an examination and exploration of several interlocking processes.

Clearing the ground

Like a builder youth workers must first clear the ground before digging foundations. Youth workers at times do important one-to-one work with a young person in crisis. It is because of the relationship that the young person seeks out an opportunity to talk, hence the need to focus the worker's thinking, to respond appropriately with what are often called *listening skills* or the *arts of conversation*. Before proceeding we need to own up to the attraction of this 'counselling' role. The counsellor appears to have a kind of gentle power, a power to probe within the internal world. Such power holds temptations. As a detached worker it certainly appealed to me! However, after subsequently training and practising as a qualified counsellor I recognised that employing counselling skills was not the same as counselling. It is an important distinction. The worker hopefully recognises that someone meeting a counsellor consciously chooses to. A young person talking to a youth worker, who uses counselling skills, is likely to think they are 'having a chat'. Awareness of the wish to think of oneself as a counsellor is a vital recognition. To do so may seem diminishing, but there is an alternative way of viewing this process. For in clearing this ground we can discover clarity. It allows us gradually to recognise our reality (as distinct from one of the fantasies we hold about ourselves). I call this process self-awareness, the gradual discovery of our true selves. *Being with another* in this way is therefore a journey of self-discovery for the worker also.

When working with an individual we must think about time span. This does not refer to the longevity of a relationship. In this area of work, what I call *being with another as a professional practitioner* may last a long or brief time span. For example, I once undertook some quite intensive individual work with a member's cousin who visited the club once. After an activity with intermittent conversation, we talked on for perhaps half an hour. No contact was continued. We are talking quality here, not quantity. It is not possible to define this way of *being with* in terms of time scale, setting or even content. Rather the task of *being with* a young person is a way of working, one held in the mind of the practitioner.

'Being with'

To dig the foundations of understanding we will consider what *being with* a young person means. Practitioners constantly look for needs, patterns and opportunities. For instance, we notice that Jason's body language is different today. He is quieter, isolated. The worker wonders if something has happened to Jason, expressed through his behaviour. The body language may be 'speaking' something he cannot put into words. The worker's awareness has been alerted. 'Keeping an eye out' is an essential part of the process of being with a young person. Growth and development are rarely on worker's minds as they seek to involve young people in activities. You are working with a group about to play a game. While choosing teams deeply held feelings emerge. A new member, Aaron, begins to express himself violently at the idea of being in a different team from his friend. The reflective practitioner looks for a way to deal with this question and the potential conflict. They note the strong feelings that have shown themselves to be a part of Aaron. An aware worker will reflect on this and collate it with other evidence about Aaron. They will keep their awareness focused on Aaron in other situations. They are beginning *to be with* Aaron in a different way. Initially such awareness frequently springs from a 'problem'. The young person says something or acts in ways that alert them. Their focus is intensified and they become differently conscious of *being with* this young person.

Awareness is the beginning for *being with* a young person, for attending to Jason or Aaron with different levels of consciousness. *Being with* is also about hunches and not knowing – a conundrum has surfaced. For in each example the worker didn't know what was happening for Jason or for Aaron. Both times they noticed something different, wondered what affected their mood and behaviour and allowed themselves to be, as Schön tells us we must, open to experiencing 'surprise, puzzlement, or confusion in a situation' that is 'uncertain or unique' (1983: 68). Here is the starting point for being with another as a professional practitioner. Once awareness is aroused by something further questions and factors emerge. Regarding Jason or Aaron the practitioner will seek to comprehend the 'behaviour' by reference to past conduct. Is there a pattern, has something similar occurred before? Do you have any information about them? Has anything happened in the family, peer group or school? Is that whisper about exclusion reliable? What about that half conversation overheard about his Dad being arrested, or sister returning home? Didn't you think his friends were unusually boisterous last night? Clues do not amount to explanations, they are just *possible* connections. I think of this as putting nuggets away, perhaps worthless today, possibly helpful tomorrow. The kinds of questions posed above concern information and fact. Essential to fill in the knowledge void, but surprise, puzzlement, confusion and uncertainty are feelings. Feelings closely associated with a lack of knowledge. Feelings that may have various emotional links and meanings associated with them for the practitioner. Making sense of, understanding, managing and using our feelings is something this chapter constantly returns to. First though it is important to revisit our examples. If it is unusual for Jason to come into the project looking as he does it is a fair bet something has happened – the natural tendency is to want to know what. However, here we encounter a fundamental principle of *being with* another person. Your focus of attention is primarily on *the experience* of the person, not on what happened. What has Aaron or Jason made of their experience? What is its meaning to them? Loosing sight of this principle is often the cause of failure in our work with an individual.

Choosing your role

Having your awareness of Jason raised does not mean you must intervene. Whether or not to act is a choice you must make. If you opt to intervene you must identify a feasible and appropriate way of doing so. For example, it may be inappropriate to publicly approach Jason. His body language may communicate 'stay away'. Therefore, you must carefully construct an opportunity for a conversation to occur. Alternatively we can approach this question of role in different way. Who are you – when you are behind the coffee bar and a young person loiters and wants to talk? Who are you – when someone turns up 'after hours' or 'bumps into you' in the street and you don't know why they have sought you out? Who are you – when you notice significant changes in behaviour or someone enters your office crying? What happens to you – when you find yourself focused on an individual? What part of you responds in these situations? You may find yourself excited by the possibility of working one-to-one with some young person, or not? Do your feelings depend on who it is and your feelings about them? You may be occupied doing the accounts or otherwise busy? You may wish to give information and move on. You may want to stop everything and focus attention on them or keep a distance? We are in the territory here of self-awareness. Judgements have to be made and responses given often in a very short time. It is therefore essential you know you have a choice. Choosing your role becomes, with practice, a conscious professional action, an element of *reflective practice*.

Choosing embraces many factors but broadly they fall within three headings: the young person, situation and yourself. Each is informed, though the questions are not all answered, through looking with care at your role. What is your role in relation to the young person? It may be the activity you are focused on can be put aside or passed on. If someone's case were an emergency, then a different choice would be made. Here we need to pay attention to the question – what is my task here and now? Answering this question goes a long way to working out your role. Making choices about your task is a constant theme for practitioners. Some situations are pressing. Tina appears in floods of tears as you prepare to go to the Juvenile Court to act as a character witness for Sam. She tells you her mother, once a part-time worker in the club, is about to leave her father. Tina is devastated and has tried to patch things up. Now her young brother has walked out of the house and 2 hours later is still missing. Clearly both Sam and Tina are important. As the worker you wish to respond to both. It may not seem questions about role are relevant here. But they are. The questions the worker asks here are – what is important, what is urgent and what is infused with the fog of strong feelings. Certainly the fog of strong feelings tends to confuse. All too easily they can energise and provoke an imperative to rush about and try to solve problems. Though Tina's brother's disappearance may be an emergency it is unlikely the state of her parent's relationship can be changed quickly. Tina, with recognition and feedback about how distressing this is, may best be employed finding her brother. They will need each other. There may also be some question about contacting her teachers depending on Tina's relationship with them. But that can wait. Tina's situation, though as important, is less urgent. Talking on Sam's behalf will not wait.

The demands on workers mean they must choose their role and *manage both the self and the situation*. So, the questions – what is my task? and what role am I in here? – help the practitioner be in the right place at the right time mentally, emotionally and physically. Had the Juvenile Court visit not been pressing and you were filing, Tina's arrival would still have prompted a question about your role, but the options and answers would be different. 'Being with' Tina would express itself through the role of a listener, a presence, a holder of strong emotions and, perhaps, the initiator of some action.

Finding the setting

Often questions arise regarding where individual work takes place. You may not have an appropriate quiet room. Counsellors meet clients in particular rooms, with door closed and interruptions excluded. This fosters a feeling that attention is focused on the client. Youth workers seldom have such rooms when required. It is a youth work skill to think about settings. Club workers are constantly shifting stuff about to enhance the setting. To encourage member interaction, to evoke a response or to have quieter games you move the furniture. Simple changes often affect behaviour, for example, to curtail the rush at opening time you open only one door or you shut the coffee bar 15 minutes early to indicate closure is near. Should you create a setting where the focus is on the young person? The closed-door intensive setting may discourage some, so a more informal space may be appropriate. These are matters of judgement and opportunities for involving young people in decision-making.

Finding the setting is a task best achieved together. The suggestion 'lets go in here?' or 'shall we go for a walk?' if taken up is a beginning. Getting a coat, a few moment's wait, perhaps some agreement about where you are going and for how long are all connections, small markers of being with each other. For a counsellor their client decides to come to them so something is already happening. For the youth worker this is less likely to be the case. The individual work, their being with another, starts further back. Making a space may be walking or finding a café. The point is to find a setting where both of you can focus on each other.

Building a working alliance

With these foundations we can begin the process of construction. As in a building there are outer walls, inner rooms, the electrical and plumbing services and the like so in the process of working with an individual there are inter-connecting elements. In finding an appropriate setting and choosing our role we build the rapport essential for *a relationship of mutual trust and emotional affinity*. Rapport is fundamental. Given the young person has accepted the setting offered and is with you to talk about something important to them suggests the initial stages of rapport are present. Usually you will have a mutual 'history'. This was the case with Jason and Tina. With Aaron the working relationship was recent, but he knew the worker's role. Similarly with regard to the cousin, who dropped in, we could 'place' each other. What was different with the last one was that in a short time we established what counsellors call a *working alliance*. This is essential but the time this takes to establish can vary greatly. It is not the same as rapport, although related. For you can have rapport with someone at a party, but that does not mean you have a *working alliance*. It is likely that with Tina, who sought out the worker when she was distressed, the working alliance will be quickly established. With Aaron and Jason it will take longer. The *working alliance* means there is a relaxation of 'defences' and that you are going to work, in your different roles, towards something that will support the young person. This is rarely explicit; it just happens the relationship reaches that stage. But of course building a *working alliance* can take considerable effort and skill; however, it is important to acknowledge the significance of 'the moment'. This is difficult to get at because it is part of the inner world. Generally people become ready to talk when they are ready. There is some inner process or order. The Greeks used the idea of logos time, the cosmic order or when things are ready (see Boardman *et al.* 1992). Logos, it must be noted, is distinguished from chronos or clock time. Without diverting into philosophy or religion there often seems a coming together of factors connecting inner and outer worlds. It is difficult to catch.

So you as a worker and the young person are together in an appropriate setting. What happens next? How do you begin? Well in a sense you have already begun. But the 'how do I begin?' question lingers. A straight question – 'Why are you in a mood, Jason?' – will probably be counterproductive. It is best young people tell their story. So the beginning is about finding ways for them to articulate their experience. Let's say you meet with Tina the next day and you may ask her 'why don't you just tell me about what has happened?' 'Open questions' requiring neither 'yes' or 'no' answers are frequently used. Regarding Jason and Aaron preparatory steps need to be taken to build a working alliance. The first is 'hearing' the unspoken communication. Both are making it clear something is not right for them. But they are unable to say so in words, they are 'saying' it in their actions. If you want to respond to this communication it is often best to use this language of action. This step, of understanding and using the same language, may rather than connect with the content of their story, make a bridge with the medium of the story. This is so often called the body language. The hunched shoulders, the head down and air of depression can be recognised ('heard') as a way of saying 'something is wrong'. How to respond? Asking the straight question – *why are you in a mood?* – closes him down because, though the question seems to be about Jason, it actually starts with where the questioner is. For it is the questioner who wants to know; therefore, this question is not really about Jason. Worse, it is likely he will experience such a question as accusatory – why are you moody? To develop a working alliance you need to start where the other is. However, Jason may not know why he feels like he does or be unable to put his feeling into words.

The starting is not to find why Jason looks as he does; that may emerge later. The initial steps must be to open channels of communication. A verbal communication that starts with where Jason is might say 'you're looking pretty fed-up, Jason'. This requires Jason to recognise, in words, how he feels. So an alternative is to communicate in the language of the body. For Jason hunched shoulders, bent head and sense of depression are his 'language'. An approach that bypasses verbal communication is, through using the same 'language', adopting Jason's posture or aspects of it – this is called *mirroring*. Here the worker's body mirrors Jason's. Body language takes a different quicker route to the brain than verbal language. Often it bypasses the conscious mind. So it would be 'heard' by Jason instantly. Words could follow – 'feeling really fed-up is horrible'. It often makes a better bridge to make a comment than asking a question. What makes this communication is not only what the worker does but the young person's response which may often itself be via body language – a relaxation or opening up of the shoulders or raising of the head. Observation is essential to discern the language and meaning of the response. The practitioner's own response is modified accordingly. Communication is thereby established.

There is no right way to achieve connection between people. It is part of the relationship. There are many different possibilities and considerable subtlety. Perhaps each relationship has a unique quality. What is common is these steps lead towards building *the working alliance*. Without the sense of joining together to work at something subsequent wise words are of no avail. While writing this chapter I encountered an example of how difficult it can be to develop a working alliance. Penny (16), who had come for an interview, said that she was leaving school because she had five siblings to look after and her mother was always criticising her. Penny said they perpetually rowed and therefore needed her own place if she was to continue studying. Getting somewhere without financial support would be difficult and perhaps undesirable. The first step, it seemed, was to work with mother and daughter about their relationship. My aim was to help her to function, as a daughter, student, sibling and young woman, within the family. I made a home visit to meet the mother. She had to empty their main room of the children and her partner, not Penny's father, to speak to me without interruption. I had the early stages of a working alliance with Penny. But I began my relationship with her mother as a male stranger, who she believed her daughter had informed she was a bad mother. This was the setting and 'being with' situation I found myself in. The starting point for our relationship was the message her daughter believed she was unsupportive. It seemed difficult not to provoke her hostility, denial or collapse. How might I establish a *working alliance* with this woman whom I barely knew and who I threatened?

First I reflected on her experience as a mother whose eldest had become stubborn and wilful. I approached building rapport and a working alliance by expressing admiration of her achievements. But I couldn't avoid the purpose of my visit. So I began by admitting that what I would be saying might be unwelcome to her and then outlined the facts of my discussion with Penny. I tried to add meaning to this in terms of the thoughts and feelings she must be having. I stressed that conflict during adolescence was commonplace. This complex communication became more difficult as English was her second language. I said I guessed she wouldn't view things as Penny did. I encouraged her to interrupt me, to express her thoughts. As we talked I watched for signs of tensing up or of softening in her face and body. What happened when I spoke of her daughter; how I perceived her position; of the impact of Penny's adolescence on her? I watched how she responded and reflected back, in précis form, what she said. Where I sensed tenseness or resistance I often gave voice to it – '*I imagine you feel hurt and perhaps angry that your daughter both feels these things and what is more speaks to me, a stranger, of you in this way?*' It was speaking to someone else of family matters that allowed her face and shoulders to relax the most. It emerged that it was the sense of shame, confusion and anger that was significant to her. Allowing this hostility towards me to emerge gave permission to give voice to these feelings. It helped us establish a rudimentary working alliance. Working with resistance this way has its root within psychoanalysis, but there is a useful way of relating it to a Gestalt perspective called supporting the resistance. The 'resistance' has its own reason for being there.

Aaron or Jason are unlikely to say how they felt, except perhaps via a verbal attack on the interrogator. So how might you match or mirror someone like them? One club worker describes how on entering the snooker room he encountered a young man cursing and hurling a snooker ball through a window. Without pausing, the worker picked up another ball, threw it through another window, shook his fist and yelled '*sometimes I get so angry I cannot find words*.' The young person immediately stopped what he was doing. What happened here can be described as mirroring in action and it worked. For communication between them was established, words were found that enabled the young man to express his anger and pain through tears (Wilson 1985).

We want deep connection with others. We like being listened to and understood. Generally building rapport begins when you begin to give your thoughtful attention to another. What we have explored above are exceptions to that experience. It is like the layer of bricks upon which everything else rests. Unlike brick foundations, however, rapport needs constant attention, and it can break down. Such things as loss of confidentiality or ignoring boundaries can overnight destroy a carefully built rapport.

Resources – using theory

To respond to the sudden aggressive demands of someone like Aaron, the silent powerful communications of Jason or the raw feelings of Penny, practitioners must draw on deep wells of resource. There are two I will comment on. One is the well of theory, the other our own emotional life. Many useful areas of theory exist. An example of drawing from this well came in the conflict between Penny and her mother. They were originally from Ghana. Part of the mother's complaint was the effect of British culture on Penny; 'when she first came here she was so different from now', she protested. Here my understanding of adolescent development helped me explain some of those changes. I recalled a section of Rayner's book entitled 'The Denigration of Parents'; subsequently I found the quote which began: 'the manic mood is not only grandiose about the self it can very readily also be disparaging of his parents and other adults' (1986: 153). Understanding this normalisation and contextualisation of the developmental process helped me support Penny's mother in her puzzlement of what was happening to them.

The well of theory also helped me understand 'resistance', a term coined by Freud. The psychoanalytic method he developed was of an unconscious life expressed through behaviour and dreams (Freud 1900). The reasons for, or connection with, earlier childhood experience were not, he argued, known by his patients; hence the unconscious was the key to unlocking the meaning of their behaviour. He interpreted this unconscious behaviour to bring it into consciousness. Resistance described the process blocking conscious psychological awareness. He later recognised that this resistance provided clues realising it 'was itself a means of reaching the repressed and unveiling the secret of the neurosis' (Laplanche and Pontalis 1973: 395). Others extended this notion. The Gestalt ideas of Perls (1947) added to our understanding suggesting that 'you know you're getting somewhere when resistance comes up'. This is an essential element in psychosynthesis – 'resistance only erupts when something is about to happen' (Young Brown 1983: 87). Whether we like it or not, it is part of an essential self which is trying to find expression. It is essentially hopeful for

> Somehow (our) resistance must be acknowledged as of value and included in our change. The old belief needs to be embraced within the new paradigm, for they hold truth (for us) as well. Paradigm shift means movement towards an expanded belief system, not the substitution of one belief for another.
>
> (*ibid.*: 88)

Resistance must be acknowledged, its role given value and theory explored. It is often possible in some way to give the resistance its own voice, its own expression.

A colleague adapts this principle in work with groups. One example concerns a game of football that threatened to get completely out of hand because the rules were constantly being broken. He began to take it much further pushing people over, picking up the ball. When the group complained he stopped, looked hurt and said 'Oh, I am sorry I thought, because of so and so and so and so, we were not obeying the rules I didn't have too. Are we going to play to rules or not?' They continued to play without rules, for a while, until it ceased to be fun. The group worked together to agree some rules. This is skilled work that draws upon the theory of supporting the resistance.

Resources – understanding and using feelings

The other deep well of resource in *being with another* is our feelings or emotions. First we must remind ourselves of two fundamentals about the inner life of feelings. One that feelings are different from thoughts; two that we have feelings about everything. In this work, however, though we will have all sorts of feelings these are put to use, almost entirely, in an indirect way. One principle is that we rarely speak of our own feelings. This is because much of the exchange is explicitly or implicitly about the feelings of the other. These are complex enough. Introducing yours would make the task of seeing where you both were impossible.

In building working alliances we begin to understand *the story* of the other. As a child, when told a story, I remember blank anticipation. My mind was free and waiting as if I found *space in my mind* for what was to come. This image *of making a space in the mind* illustrates what happens next in being with another as a professional. Here we must allow the story to unfold. We each have our own unique story comprising the events of our lives and the way we experience and try to make sense of them over time. *Being with* someone, in the sense that I mean, involves gradually gathering up aspects of this combination of events and understandings so a sense of their uniqueness unfolds. We make links here with the engagement process. We are engaging with another. An engineering metaphor may help explain what is happening. When a cogwheel engages with another cog precisely the right space has been engineered to accept the cog so it can 'fit', move it on and do its work. Something similar happens in being with another in one-to-one working. There is space in the worker's mind not 'filled up' with the anticipated issues, required knowledge and right answers. The worker doesn't know what the young person wants to talk about. Of course the worker may, from previous encounters, have an idea, but it is a guess. They don't know how they will tell their story or what part concerns them now. Their position is of 'not knowing' and it is very important the worker views this encounter as new territory. They need space in their mind for what is coming, for both the facts of the situation and *emotional space*. There is a deep interest in the 'facts', whatever the component parts of the story are, and the feelings that accompany the telling. These two themes – the facts and the feelings – inter-relate and sometimes blend together but must be understood by the practitioner, as distinct. In following the story both facts and feelings need to make sense, to add up. Where it does not generally, it is because feelings have got caught up in it some-where. The practitioner needs to receive the sometimes strong and often contradictory feelings the young person has about the situation they are describing.

Recently when I was observing a Connexions Personal Advisor hear-ing an asylum seeker talk about a course she was undertaking it became apparent to me that he was acquiring the facts but was ignoring the young woman's feelings about the course. As a result there was disconnection in their exchange. In discussing the session afterwards I drew two par-allel lines, one headed emotions and the other practical or intellectual learning. I described these moving happily along beside each other until something happens to one of them. I then drew the emotion's line splay-ing out into the intellectual sphere. For if the emotional track of a person's life is disregarded then it will try to make sure its presence is felt in some other way. So in hearing a story both the facts and the feelings need to be listened to and given feedback. 'Space in the mind' allows the story and feelings about these events to be heard, taken in and recognition given. Then the young person has found their voice, begun saying what is going on for them and experienced being heard. Experiencing someone really listening to you and conveying what they understand is powerful. It alone can lead to change, but even if that were not so, the significance of it remains for the young person. Counsellors call this process 'summaris-ing' or 'reflecting back' the outlines or a paraphrase of the main point. Repeating key phrases or words often does the trick. With skill offering a metaphor or an image of what is said can aid the process.

Pressure to act

Often alongside 'the story' we hear a demand for change. When Penny explained the conflict with her mother she demanded I find her some-where to live. Regarding Aaron and his behaviour there was powerful pressure to stop things deteriorating and maintain discipline. In some settings it is desirable to 'jump on things quick'. Practitioners also, for example, have responsibilities to other users, colleagues and equipment. Recently I felt I had to do something to stop Simon breaking chairs. But I could also see his sadness. This sense of something being wrong applies to all my examples and so the seemingly natural response is to try to make things better, and to take away painful or angry feelings. Here we are at that other well of resource – our own feelings. We must recognise this 'pressure to act' gets inside us – I call it 'the DSN moment'. The *do something now* (DSN) state of mind compels us to change the situation. Recognising it is central to preventing it taking over. I had an overwhelming feeling I must stop Simon vandalising the room. Had I tried to stop him using equal force (if that was possible) who knows what further aggression and violence might have been unleashed. But I glimpsed in time something of the desperate pain and anger being expressed through his actions. Consequently my DSN moment was checked, replaced by a tentative desire to connect with where Simon was in his emotional state.

In conclusion

We have explored a part of professional practice that is about learning and support, developing awareness, growth and development, and relationships. We can usefully call this part of the process of 'gathering their story'. We have difficulty understanding others from inside our own skins. But we can, if we allow ourselves to have *space in our mind*, get a working understanding of someone else in relationship to particular issues. We must grasp it as an unfolding story, with always another chapter to follow. So we approach this process of being with another with awe and anticipation. Others have expressed this idea, but one that hits the spot for me is Taylor who expresses the place of the listener in this way – 'And so we enter dialogue with the humblest kind of curiosity in which expectancy and reverence and dread all have their place' (1971: 8). Humility, curiosity, expectancy, reverence and dread are pretty sound attitudes with which to approach 'being with another'. Interestingly Taylor, from a different background, comes up with a list similar to that of Schön (1983). Though 'dread' may seem a little extreme, except maybe in a case of bereavement, for example, if we see ourselves as gathering another's story in working with an individual young person with humble curiosity, expectancy and reverence we will not go far wrong.

5 'The cultivation of gifts in all directions': thinking about purpose

Dod Forrest

What should be the main purposes of youth work? In this chapter, Dod Forrest addresses this question by presenting a model of youth work as a process that links personal development, group work, collective association and social movements for radical change. While, like earlier chapters, this stresses the importance of relationships it also emphasises the place of community in young people's lives and the need for youth work to possess a social action dimension.

The perspective adopted in this chapter is in opposition to dominant contemporary models of control and socialisation. It advocates in opposition to these a civic role for young people that treats them as 'citizens not subjects' and endeavours to 'cultivate gifts in all directions' as an antidote to the alienation, anomie and individualisation that are the hallmark of capitalist societies.

It is a truism that young people in the United Kingdom live in a rapidly changing world. Over the past two decades there have been significant changes in family circumstances, the labour market, leisure patterns, lifestyle, communications and levels of dependence and independence. All of which seriously impact on the transition from childhood to adulthood. This is an era when this transition has been extended further into the life cycle than ever before. The shift of responsibility for the welfare of young people from the state to the family, coupled with structural unemployment, has created pressures, especially for young people from working-class backgrounds, which have increased the incidence of suicide, depression, eating disorder and self-harm (Furlong and Cartmel

1997; Bradshaw and Mayhew 2005). In this context, the purpose of youth work is a question that goes to the heart of the working relationship between workers and young people. In this chapter I will argue that the purpose of youth work must be understood within the context of an alienating and individualising society. I have adopted the classic definition of alienation given by Marx in his *Economic and Philosophic Manuscripts* to elucidate this process. Although this definition addresses the plight of the labourer in capitalist society I suggest a wider interpretation, one that embraces all social relationships of labour – in the school, community and home environments. For Marx:

> the product of labour is alienation, production itself must be active alienation, the alienation of activity, the activity of alienation... labour is external to the worker, i.e. it does not belong to his essential being;... in his work therefore, he does not affirm himself but denies himself, does not feel content but unhappy, does not develop freely his mental and physical energy but mortifies his body and ruins his mind.
>
> (1963: 72)

There is one antidote to this loss of a creative 'inner world' as identified above and it is 'community' – but not just any community. Marx and Engels' (1994) discussion of 'individuals, class and community' in *The German Ideology* point to a perspective on regaining humanity still pertinent to contemporary struggles for dignity, assertiveness and freedom. Within this real 'oppositional community' there is a challenge to the core market and profit-driven values of our society for they argue,

> Only in community with others has each individual the means of **cultivating his gifts in all directions**; only in the community, therefore, is personal freedom possible... individuals find their freedom in and through their association.
>
> (*ibid*.: 83)

A more recent account of the development of the phenomenon of alienation is offered by Beck (1992, 2005). He theorises that a process of 'individualisation' is identifiable as one of the contours associated with changing social relationships in the family and at work. In this respect he detects a loss of the traditional solidarity of the old industrial society, one dominated by identification with class and community. In the more pluralistic society, which has taken its place, the changing composition of the family, precipitated by gender and sexuality factors on the one hand, and new work patterns on the other, becomes a key issue facing a new generation of young people and their parents. However, in relation to this context of rapid change, within what Beck terms the 'risk society', some things remain constant. The neighbourhood you live in will still significantly determine whether you are likely to stay on at school or even attend school on a regular basis (Power 2007). Gender, race, sexuality and disability all increase vulnerability to discrimination and prejudice and health will vary according to your family income (Griffin 1993; Office of National Statistics 2006). It may be true that young people today are born into an era of what Giddens (1990) terms late industrialism but it remains an era characterised by social inequalities – of rich and poor, poverty and inequality – a world dominated still by social class, sexism, racism and war.

What is identified by Beck is a changing apparatus of power in the contemporary era, a shift in the levers of control and domination by those who wield power through exploitation and oppression worldwide. He suggests the relationship between the individual, family and community is undermined by powerful institutions:

> ... the place of traditional ties and social forms (social class, nuclear family) is taken by secondary agencies and institutions, which stamp the biography of the individual and make that person dependent upon fashions, social policy, economic cycles and markets, contrary to the image of individual control which establishes itself in consciousness.
>
> (1992: 131)

Within this process of individualisation and fragmentation there is emerging a more reflexive younger generation, a generation which, 'on reflection', has challenged the enduring inequalities of so-called modernity and as one commentator has identified:

> The result is reflected not simply in macro-processes such as the re-birth of feminism and the progressive incorporation of women into the labour market, but also in the micro-struggles between individual women and men as they seek to redefine their personal relationships.
>
> (Callinicos 1999: 300)

In opposition to a process of individualisation there has also been a flowering of critique, and the growth of new forms of association that have generated an influential undercurrent of questioning, challenge and re-appraisal. The rise of oppositional social movements in Europe and around the world has been a testament to a new different and assertive form of politics. And young people have from the onset been at the centre of this development. These groups seek to challenge the symptoms of the risk society that is, pollution, disease, poverty, racism and war, through the formation of new social movements for progressive change (Scott 1990; Freire 1996; Klein 2000; Bircham and

Charlton 2001; Dee 2004). For example, the growth of a new global community, meeting under the umbrella of the World Social Forum, and an increasing number of Regional Social Forums advocating 'Another World Is Possible' has emerged to become a substantial political influence.

If we enter into an empowering relationship with young people we can contribute to this process of personal reflexivity and direct action for local and global social change. We can 'cultivate gifts in all directions' by linking local activism to global issues. At a local level there are now numerous examples of young people's involvement in a multiplicity of serious issues and campaigns. Scotland's 'Show Racism a Red Card' has been promoted by teachers in many secondary schools. Fair trade initiatives in schools are on the increase as witnessed by the work of the Montgomery Development Education Centre in Aberdeen, and other centres throughout the United Kingdom, supported by Oxfam, that have led to some small-scale investigations of purchasing policy and links with schools and villages in Africa. Anti-war protests have been supported by young people, as illustrated by the large numbers of Scottish school students who staged walkouts and strikes on the day that the invasion of Iraq took place during March 2003. Issues of environmental justice are now central to many citizenship initiatives in schools and youth projects attracting membership of Friends of the Earth groups, projects and campaigns, alongside a growing network of World Development Movement associations at a local level.

Models of youth work

Furlong *et al.* (1997) suggest that historically there have been four models of youth work and arguably these can still be identified within different settings today. The four models they categorise are:

- *Control*: Young people are viewed as a threat to society; they are perceived as disconnected and dangerous. Policies such as the introduction of Anti Social Behaviour Orders (ASBOs) and curfews as well as the growing employment of community wardens linked to the local policing of neighbourhoods all reflect an expansion of this approach;
- *Socialisation*: Within this model young people are deemed to be in need of rescue for their own good. This view of youth work is often provoked by periodic 'moral panics' associated with teenage pregnancy, drug-taking and vandalism. This is a problem-centred focused

youth work and parents and young people are increasingly identified as 'the problem';

● *Informal education*: This form of youth work draws on a philosophy of liberal education. Young people are assisted to be critical and questioning of adults, especially those in positions of authority and power;

● *Citizenship*: This model of youth work is comparatively new. Young people are offered political and social education through both extra-curricular activities in schools and projects in the community.

It is argued that control and socialisation models are features of more traditional club-based work, and the newer drugs prevention, community safety, young unemployed and mentoring 'projects' are more concerned with informal education and citizenship. Brown *et al.* (1995) are among those who argue this case distinguishing between '*traditional*' and '*new sector*' provision. Suggesting that

> whereas the established sector is characterised by uniformity, the new sector is characterised by diversity ... traditional concerns with building centred youth provision are replaced by issue-based concern with problems of a perceived marginality of young people, in particular, lack of space and community safety. (p. 15)

They go on to stress that this '*new sector*' is more likely to encourage young people to use computers; to engage with video, radio, music and drama; and to address issues of racism, gender, sexuality, disability and health. In my view this is a false distinction. A better, more illuminating distinction is to define youth work as an activity located in an environment under the control of young people and is premised on a voluntary relationship with a youth worker acting as a facilitator in an empowering relationship.

On closer inspection much '*new sector*' work can be seen to be targeted at those defined as being 'social problems', for example, pregnant young women, young unemployed, drug users and the rowdy. All too often '*new sector*' provision is founded upon values that have departed from youth work that embraces an informal education perspective. Smith (2002b) summarised this development with reference to government plans for the English youth services. He suggests,

> The emphasis on surveillance and control, case management, and on individualised ways of working, run counter to the key characteristics of youth work. There is a shift from voluntary participation to more coercive forms, from association to individualised activity, from education to case management

(and not even casework) and from informal to bureaucratic relationships. Significantly, there are now targets surrounding accreditation that inevitably accelerate the movement away from informal education towards formal education and formation. (p. 13)

In contrast an empowering model can generate an environment where young people create their own form of communication and association among each other and with sympathetic adults. Ironically, this educational experience appeals to some of the most disaffected and alienated young people in both working-class and middle-class communities and therefore can be a vehicle for another form of social control and socialisation, if in these youth work settings key values are not made explicit.

Participation and partnership can become a controlling agenda, especially in a setting that fails to challenge racism, normative gender relations, and discrimination on grounds of disability and sexuality. Radical forms of youth work, which is a new sector, whether on the street, within an Internet café or as part of a citizenship project that offers control of resources and programmes, can also mask a controlling and conservative environment. Two examples spring to mind. Some work with girls- and boys-only groups offer no challenge to gender stereotyping. In a similar vein, some white-only areas or youth work settings can be deemed to have no problems with racism. These are complex issues of power as well as empowerment and they are addressed later in this chapter.

One person's empowerment is often another's loss of power. In the micro processes of decision making in a youth work setting, what is not on the agenda for discussion is perhaps more important than what is, for non-decision making (Crenson 1971) is the most prolific and potent form of power. If the item is not on the formal or informal agenda, it doesn't become open to challenge and debate. It cannot be changed.

Thus central to these values must be a commitment to autonomy, democracy and accountability and justice. According to Kieffer (1984) engagement with community activists that embodies these values can create a more positive self – concept for the person and increased competence. It can also generate a more critical and analytical understanding of the social and political environment. However, informal education is only possible within a setting that offers young people realistic levels of control, participation and power.

The following section offers a personal account of youth work intervention and a case study of one intervention developed at my place of work.

Youth work as informal education: a reflexive account

Some youth workers I recall with respect and affection. They introduced me to something new in my life – an idea, experience, opinion or issue they felt passionately about, a piece of music, tale of their journey abroad or photograph of another part of the world. Also they treated me as a person with something worthwhile to contribute and were able to listen and not judge. They introduced me to something different from home and school, where travel and literature were restricted by low income. Some were Christians and this triggered an intense interest in religion and spirituality that persists to this day. Others were sceptics acquainting me to doubt in the world and the literature of criticism, opposition and revolution. These youth workers were the first adults out with family and school to engage in this kind of conversation. They managed to nurture and develop the working-class milieu I inhabited – bringing jazz, religion, books and politics into my life. Collectively they created a youth club where we 'had a say' about the music, had our own table space and participated on our terms – devising our programme of social activities.

Somehow schoolteachers had never succeeded in engaging with me in this kind of conversation or dialogue. Schoolteachers were paid to 'teach' me and I was obliged to listen. Although some managed to arouse within me a great interest in particular subjects, particularly poetry, overall they never felt able to reveal a bit of their own selves, their strengths and weaknesses in a way that allowed their humanity to emerge. By way of contrast the youth workers surrendered a glimpse of their values, shared their particular interests, showed a willingness to give up time to help organise an event or come with us to some tiny residential centre in the back or beyond. Somehow they conveyed a genuine interest in our view of events and issues – the events and issues important to us at the time. However, the workers were not passive for each had an ability to listen and challenge in a youth club designed and structured to accommodate informal group discussion. The environment was under our control because it comprised no more than a table that squeezed 10 to 15 of us around it during an evening. Here was space we managed, which allowed relationships within our group to mature and flourish – fostering drama in the form of love, hate, violence, marriage, sex, music and politics. Nor did these workers moralise about our drinking and getting drunk; gambling and losing money; indulging in under-age sex and getting pregnant. Yet within these troubled times for many help, support, advice and assistance were integral to the relationship of trust and reciprocity that grew between the workers and the group. In contemporary terms the relationship might be termed 'natural mentoring' (Philip 2003); we merely saw it as warm, welcoming and worthwhile. The ethos of this club identified fighting and stealing as wrong. But then, as now, around the world it was obvious wars were taking place. We debated and questioned why some people were forced to fight and sometimes riot, why the theft of resources from poor nations by rich ones never seemed to be viewed as wrong or illegal. Such encounters formed some of my core values. Upon reflection I could depict this relationship between the members and workers as an empowering one. This form of empowerment assumes a zero-sum view of power. In this zero-sum definition of power, one person's empowerment is another's loss of power. This view of power is in contrast to a perspective which assumes an ever-increasing expansion of power that does not alter the status, control and management by the powerful. In a zero-sum world of powerful and powerless, power is a social relationship (Lukes 2005) and thus the social content of empowerment practice should ensure a less controlling youth worker. It must also allow for young people publicly criticising the workers' employers and funders and questioning and lobbying governments and others.

Nowadays youth work, especially in the state sector, is more centralised and practice more closely scrutinised. Resources, staffing, funding and premises are all more likely to be targeted upon those deemed a problem to themselves and society. Should we abandon universality, disregard those who are 'not a public nuisance'? Should workers set aside the need to introduce as many elements of informal education to as wide an audience as possible? I think not. For as my experiences and the following case studies exemplify we must attempt to develop empowering youth work relationship for all young people.

Techno teenagers: a case study of an empowering approach to youth work

This case study, written up in more detail elsewhere (Forrest and Wood 1999; Wood and Forrest 2000), illustrates the work of an action research youth project that sought to prevent harm to young people by offering them opportunities to develop their musical and media interests. The project aimed to involve them in decision making and foster participation in a democratic process of programme planning and evaluation. Based at Mastrick Community Centre in the north of Aberdeen and funded by the Scottish Office in the mid-1990s it became the starting point for a decade of youth work development in the locality. The first year of the project evolved through various stages of development. The initial phase brought together small groups whose discussions subsequently formed the basis of tutor-led workshops in dance and DJ'ing. A summer programme built on other identified interests organised football, fishing, golf, music, a writers' group and advice sessions. These interests eventually narrowed to become in-depth work with girls involved in a writing group and boys who organised a series of raves at the Centre and received football coaching. A final phase sought to develop peer education through discussions of health and drugs and the girls group of writers published three issues of the *Mastrick Magazine* that featured discussions of these issues and many more. Key themes that became the focus of worker intervention were the relationship between the young men and women; women's rights to DJ'ing and rave event organisation; and general involvement in programme planning.

It was during the first year that links were established with Save the Children's Article 12 organisation that was formed to promote Article 12 of the UN Convention on the Rights of the Child, and the idea of a local youth café for the sole use of young people was first discussed. My role as youth worker was influenced by the educational philosophy of Paulo Freire, and theories of empowerment and action research that sought to involve young people. These influences were translated into the following practices:

● Formation of a youth advisory panel bringing together young people, workers and Community Education Centre management representatives;
● Introduction of the 'open meeting' that is, an invitation to all young people to participate in the setting of the programme agenda for a 10-week block;
● Formation of a 'Rave Committee'. This group of teenagers was elected by their peers to represent the interests of the rave music followers in the area;
● Introduction after a period of debate of the 50 per cent ruling. For example, the Rave Committee had to have at least 50 per cent female membership;
● A 'looking back' meeting whereby the advisory panel reviewed the successes and failures of the previous 10-week programme;
● A decision to work with certain young women through a writing and magazine project.

Drugs issues and educational sessions were introduced when they grew out of the work with the young people. The interest in raves and techno music came from those who were travelling to clandestine music events in the North East of Scotland. Specialist organisations equipped to handle serious drugs and alcohol use were brought in to compliment the work undertaken by the workers. Advice giving became a growing feature of the work as young people sought help over such concerns as financial matters, jobs, housing and getting into trouble. It was significant that the project attracted young women in their late teens, possibly more by accident than design. These, it subsequently emerged, were particularly attracted by the opportunity to be involved in magazine production and discussion groups.

Young women writers' group

It is perhaps significant that *Sophie's World* (Gaarder 1995), a mystery story that seeks to illustrate the key traditions of western philosophy, was for a brief period in the early 1990s among the most popular books among young people in Europe. I have consistently found within the context of my practice that young people are passionately interested in why the world is the way it is, and what might be termed 'the world of ideas'. Yet they are rarely given the opportunity to philosophise, argue and discuss issues that are central to their lives. The members of the writers' group who produced *The Mastrick Magazine* were friends of the young men attracted to the project by the offer of being able to learn and practice their music and meet well-known city DJs. These young women came into the centre one night and having failed to get a 'turn on the decks' were persuaded to join the first meeting of the magazine group. In this preliminary session the group were asked to complete a number of unfinished sentences such as – I wonder why . . .? The thing that makes me really angry is . . . I think it is wrong that . . . The responses to these prompts posed for their readers in the first issue of the magazine a number of challenging questions:

> Why are we brought up the way we are? I mean we grow up, go to school, work, have kids and get married – why? I often wonder why life has gone past so quick and I wonder why we do things we regret later and why we have to take responsibility at a young age. I often wonder why life is the way it is and why it is so hard sometimes. Have you ever wondered why bad things happen to the kindest of people?

These young people were angered by racism; pollution of the environment; the deaths of some of their closest friends from drug taking; their exclusion from the DJ'ing and rave music project; and the local policing practice of 'moving them on'. The main concerns they identified and wanted to discuss and write about were:

- Coping with bereavement;
- Spiritualism;
- Their right as young women to be treated with respect and equality;
- To learn more about 'green' issues;
- How to change police behaviour.

The purpose of youth work: 'cultivating gifts in all directions'

Studies of empowerment (Rappaport *et al.* 1984), especially the work of Kieffer (1984), identify a paradox, one evident in the work undertaken with these young people. Many who became involved in the life of the project were among those most alienated from school, work and home. One young member of the magazine group had been expelled from the local secondary school and had been part of the crowd hanging around the local precinct most nights. This is her account of why the writing project was important:

> I like it because I like being part of something, part of a team and my opin-
> ions and ideas being heard. It gives me something to speak about, like at job
> interviews. Something I've done, something I'm part of...
>
> (cited in Wood and Forrest 2000: 72)

Another member described the experience in these terms:

> It proved we could do something. It felt great seeing my name on the paper.
> I've never done anything like that before. I really like writing.
>
> (cited in Forrest and Wood 1999: 9)

Kieffer describes empowerment as a process, which generates 'participatory competence'. By this he means gaining a more positive self-concept and sense of self-competence, a construction of a more critical and analytical understanding of your social and political environment and the cultivation of individual and collective resources for social and political action. In this respect he found a key link in this process 'chain' were those adults who adopted the role of mentor in the dialogical relationship described by Freire (1976). Youth work at Mastrick was modelled on this relationship. Freire (1976: 41) described this dialogical relationship in these terms:

> *Through this project* [The Adult Education Project of the Movement of Popu-
> lar Culture, Recife] we launched a new institution of popular culture, a 'culture

circle', since among us a school was a traditionally passive concept. Instead of a teacher, we had a co-ordinator; instead of lectures, dialogue; instead of pupils, group participants; instead of alienating syllabi, compact programs that were 'broken down' and 'codified' into learning units. The topics for debate were offered us by the groups themselves . . . nationalism, profit remittances abroad, the political evolution of Brazil, development, illiteracy, the vote for illiterates, democracy were some of the themes which were repeated from group to group.

Acknowledgement of the interest and aspirations of young people is potentially the greatest contribution to empowerment. Many of them want to change the world for the better. We should assist them in this endeavour. After all as an old philosopher now enjoying a resurgence of interest in his writings explained '. . . philosophers have only interpreted the world in various ways, but the real task is to change it' (Marx 1970: 123).

Protest problematises the world. It begins by seeking answers to 'why?' questions and it is the starting point of what Freire terms 'conscientisation' − '. . . a process of humanisation through the development of a critical consciousness (1976: 16). A youth worker can assist a process of conscientisation by going to the young people and helping them to enter the historical process critically. As Ferguson (1982: 24) points out, it allows people generally to develop confidence and take action collectively:

. . . to come to a conscious realisation that their situation is neither inevitable or natural but caused by social processes which can be reversed whenever the mass of ordinary people act together against them.

Kieffer (1984) suggests the empowerment process proceeds via four distinct stages:

- The era of entry;
- The era of advancement;
- The era of incorporation;
- The era of commitment.

The initial impetus for change is the era of entry, and he suggests that this is generated by 'tangible and direct threats to individual or familial self-interests' (*ibid*.: 18). He found that it is only when a 'sense of integrity is directly violated or attacked that these individuals respond' (*ibid*.: 18).

The starting point for work with the girls was their anger at the injustice of never getting 'a turn on the decks' and having no involvement in the decision making that planned the choice of DJs and the organisation of rave music events at the Centre. When these issues were coupled with more complex issues of bereavement, spirituality, racism, the environment and local policing this became a powerful setting for dialogue to take place within. The girls discussed and debated these issues with youth workers alongside a series of invited speakers comprising an educational psychologist, a priest, the community 'bobby', a local anti-racist activist from the Racial Equality Council and an environmentalist. These discussions were then written about and became the source for magazine material.

According to Kieffer the period of entry merges into an era of advancement that featured:

● The centrality of a mentoring relationship;
● Supportive peers within a collective organisational structure;
● Cultivation of a more critical understanding of social and political relations.

The person described as the mentor, external enabler or the outside community organiser, as recorded in the lives of the community activists that were interviewed by Kieffer, was a key influence. This person was described by one of the community activists he interviewed as follows:

> when I first got involved . . . the (local organizers) all saw beyond me . . . they just didn't see me. They saw what I was capable of, what I could be . . . . It was so important that somebody cared enough to be there encouraging me, pushing me . . . coming back after me . . . no matter how afraid I was.
>
> (*ibid.*: 20)

The role of youth worker as identified in the 'Techno Teenagers' project was exactly as described above. It was the ability to see beyond the girls who were not challenging boyfriends and peers and embrace the belief that these girls would, with support and encouragement, be very capable writers and DJs, that cemented this youth work relationship.

A third phase of 'incorporation' is described by Kieffer as a time of consolidation on the one hand and on the other a realisation that powerful vested interests are resistant to change. It is during this period that '. . . organising skills are sharpened, leadership skills honed and survival skills, of necessity, are constructed' (*ibid.*: 22). It was during this time that members of the girls group met with the local community police officers and wrote to the chief constable complaining about police behaviour and then presented their case for more resources to the local councillor, community council and the Centre's management body. Also during this time the magazine was circulated widely in the local community.

Ultimately, there is a final phase of development of an 'era of commitment' and widening of opportunities. As two participants in the Kieffer study put it,

... my values have changed. My priorities have changed. Everything has changed ... people can't really learn the things that I've learned, through workshops or through classes or courses ... you have to experience it yourself to really know.

(*ibid*.: 24)

The development of learning about self and the world opens up incalculable opportunities in terms of relationships, jobs and study.

All the girls in the writers' group moved on to employment and training. One of the main organisers of the group became an Article 12 worker for Aberdeen and was a central figure in the campaign which subsequently emerged to fund an independent youth café under the managerial control of young people in Mastrick. A fund-raising effort by a new generation of young people produced in excess of £100,000. In 2000 a Mastrick Youth Café opened in a recently closed local police sub station and is now known as The Box. The 4 years of fund-raising, planning and design of the premises – all facilitated by youth workers – is another story, still to be told.

In conclusion: an empowering approach to work with young people

Empowerment begins with a process of personal empowerment that has been defined as

the process whereby the individual feels increasingly in control of their own affairs and ... for them to be in control is a pre-requisite for them to feel they can help someone else.

(Lord and Farlow 1990: 3)

The link between personal control and offering support to others gives a clue to an important process of educational development associated with personal empowerment. It is perhaps instructive to note that the next generation of part-time youth workers and volunteers in the Mastrick area has drawn on young people involved during this particular phase of youth work development.

A collective understanding of a problem is essentially related to an individual process of empowerment. The work of Mullender and Ward (1991) suggests that we can assist a process of collective empowerment by facilitating a form of self-directed group work. However, as they explain,

> groups are not fully empowering if... they stop short at providing only a source of mutual help and support, or at simply lamenting shortfalls or failings in services... valuable as support may be, it does not help participants to generalise from their particular situation to wider social processes. (p. 161)

A level of collective empowerment seeks to problematise the world, and to activate individuals into challenging existing social policies and political decisions (see Richardson 2008). To paraphrase C. Wright Mills (1959), it is about turning personal problems into issues of public concern. This level of empowerment seeks the transformation of existing institutions. In this setting, personal attitudes and organisational goals are challenged to become anti-racist and non-sexist; and there is an opening up of traditionally male, middle-class hierarchies into opportunities for the advancement of women, black people and disabled people, through a more equitable sharing of resources for the poor.

The growth of new social movements is arguably a feature of the contest over power taking place globally and reflects contemporary debates on the meaning of empowerment. As Wallerstein points out,

> The definition of empowerment most commonly cited... has focused on changing only the subjective nature of powerlessness, with individuals treated as separate from their social contexts.
>
> (1993: 218–219)

However, as Rappaport notes,

> Our task as researchers, scholars and professionals should be to unpack and influence contemporary resolutions of paradox and that to do this we need to be more of a social movement than a profession... a social policy which views people as complete human beings, creates a symbolic sense of urgency... At this time in our history I believe that empowerment encapsulates the symbolic message required to bring a new sense of urgency.
>
> (1981: 1–2)

In a world where education has become yet another commodity to be bought and sold on the open market (see Smith 2002a) it is essential we bring this new sense of urgency to the working relationship we establish between young people and ourselves as youth workers. The antidote to a process of privatisation, alienation and individualisation within youth work is collective association, informal education and protest. We can assist this process by ensuring that our institutions are democratic. It is vital that our values of social justice, equality and equity are paramount and that we are on the side of young people who want to inhabit their own space on street corners, youth clubs, commercial establishments, workplaces and schools. This will mean assisting dialogue in relation to developments such as ASBOs, curfews, heavy-handed policing, frightened neighbours, racism, sexism and homophobia. If this dialogue turns to protest, direct action and young people's involvement in social movements then youth workers will have to follow.

6 | Programmes, programming and practice

Ruth Gilchrist

In this chapter sustained attention is paid to the content, structure and, above all, the centrality of the programme within youth work. The previous chapter discussed ways in which young people can engage with the process of developing programmes of activities. Here Ruth Gilchrist considers how this can be encouraged and the challenges this poses for youth workers in various settings.

In *Reckoning with Youth*, a classic youth work text, Anne Armson and Stanley Turnbull (1944: 23) said, 'The club programme is the scaffolding around which the whole structure is built.' This generally remains the case. Just as a detached worker must create a routine and persona that allows young people to both find and approach them so, for much the same reasons, club and project workers must pay careful attention to programme content. For it is the programme that initially draws many young people into contact with the worker, and frequently it will be the quality of the programme that determines how long such contact is sustained. Good programmes help sustain relationships, while poor ones lead to their disconnection. Fundamentally an effective programme focuses on the expressed and felt needs of potential and existing 'members'. In other words it offers those activities and encounters young people tell workers (and each other) they want. These – the expressed needs – usually include sporting opportunities, trips, computer games and 'enjoyment'. But an effective programme should not overlook the frequently unvoiced but felt needs of young people and here we are referring, for example, to the chance to make friends, share problems, resolve tensions and secure advice. The need to attend to both expressed and felt needs means constructing a programme can never be simplistically left to the 'customers'; the youth worker must be prepared as an educator, and, one might add, as an adult to intervene in order to ensure that the unspoken needs of the shy, awkward and as yet unaffiliated are taken into account. This means they must negotiate and endeavour to create programmes that are socially and educationally balanced; offer young people opportunities to be both adults and 'teenagers'; and are predictable and safe, yet challenging and developmental. Given such countervailing pressures it is little wonder that programme planning has always been a difficult, if at times neglected, task, even art.

Any discussion regarding the importance of programme planning inevitably strays into the realms of content. Armson and Turnbull (1944: 24) recommend that a good programme will incorporate a mix of activities and inputs falling within three headings – Physical, Mental and Spiritual. These are the categories that echo the essential core identified by the first national and international youth organisation, the YMCA, a hundred years earlier, a core that sought to focus on Mind, Body and Spirit. Once allowance is made for changes in the way we now describe such things, it is astonishing how much current documentation relating to the priorities and purposes of youth work continues to embrace these categories. For example, Pauline Riley (2001: 148) reported that, at the time of writing, the Cheshire and Wirral Federation of Youth Clubs aimed 'to help young people so to develop their physical, mental and spiritual capacities that they may grow to full maturity as individuals and members of society'. Much consistency remains regarding content but it is important to acknowledge from the outset that profound changes are afoot and, in particular, programmes are increasingly being shaped by external factors that are pulling in new directions.

First, funders are increasingly imposing packaged learning upon projects and clubs. As a pre-condition for the provision of funding workers are being required to focus on particular topics, for example, health education, safe sex, anger management or the raising of self-esteem. This is partly because funders do not trust workers to undertake the preparation and self-education to ensure they will 'deliver' the correct facts and the prioritised information. But also it is to enable the external agency to monitor the quality of 'delivery' and assess outcomes, something made far easier by the production of pre-packaged materials and 'recommended' forms of delivery'.

Second, funders and local and central government agencies are insisting that workers 'deliver' measured outcomes – awards, National Vocational Qualifications (NVQs) and such like. In other words, many youth workers, just like schoolteachers, are obliged to operate in ways designed to ensure young people are driven towards acquiring accredited outcomes rather than engaging in open and negotiated educational encounters. However, although state-funded youth clubs and projects may be increasingly constrained as to how they assemble a programme they still possess substantial freedom albeit generally far less than colleagues operating in settings funded and linked to voluntary and faith-based agencies.

Uniqueness of youth work

What has historically made youth clubs and projects unique as an educational experience is that they operate in radically different ways to the schools, colleges and workplaces the young people spend so much time in. Curricula, syllabi and timetables are the bedrock upon which the school experience is built. Each provides a framework within which schoolteachers operate. The timetable divides up the school day, week and year distributing the allotted time according to what the managers consider to be most beneficial for the pupils (or conducive towards the smooth-running of the institution). The first two itemise what is to be taught (and hopefully learnt) and identify the starting point and culmination of the learning experience. Within a school setting the content of both a curriculum and a syllabus is now usually imposed on teacher and students alike by government-appointed bodies such as curriculum councils and examination boards. These variously compile the syllabus, or list of requirements for passing a particular examination, and construct the curriculum, the course of study to be followed, leaving the teacher to obediently deliver the packages. Alternatively both can be negotiated. With the teacher and students collaborating to assemble the syllabus and curriculum, and even the mode of delivery of each, however, although frequently discussed (see, for example, Stenhouse 1980; Newman and Ingram 1989; McKernan 2008), this negotiated curriculum is rarely encountered within the school and college system. For in contemporary Britain, as indeed for most of the preceding two centuries, neither schoolteachers nor pupils are trusted to structure the content of the curriculum or the means by which it is 'delivered'. Rather someone up the chain of command tells the former what (and how) to teach and the latter what they must learn (Griffith 2000). Therefore both march in a pre-ordained direction to a mandated drumbeat. Historically the relative freedom of youth work from such constraints has helped set it apart from the educational mainstream.

Traditionally clubs and projects have been places where attendance is on a voluntary basis, the young people being free to come and go as they pleased. Even most of the adults are there out of choice rather than because they are paid to be in attendance. Voluntarism means youth work and youth workers have since the earliest beginnings been obliged to develop discreet ways of operating. The adults wish to educate and teach the young people but they have scrupulously avoided being designated teachers – opting instead to be known as leaders, workers, ministers or secretaries. Partly because they do not wish to be tarred with the brush of compulsion but also because they have created a different educational tradition, a *modus operandi* that sets them apart from the schoolteacher and college lecturer. Like schools and colleges clubs, projects or troops, call them what you like, are places where formal and informal education mingle. However, the balance between the two is reversed. Whereas in schools and colleges informal education intrudes into the gaps in the timetable and curriculum, occurring largely 'beyond the classroom' in break times, during lunch and before and after lessons (Hazler 1998; Luxmoore 2000; Jeffs 2007), in the youth work setting the informal is the dominant educational model. Here the formal 'lesson' is slotted into an environment overwhelmingly structured to cultivate and foster opportunities for informal educational encounters. The prime reason for this reversal is not difficult to unearth; fundamentally it is the inevitable by-product of attendance being voluntary. Managers and funders may not be happy with voluntary attendance as this makes it difficult to control what the young people learn and who they learn from, namely, their peers as well as the workers, but they can do little about this. Therefore rather than youth work being dominated and shaped by curricula, syllabi and timetables it has historically been constructed around the potentially more democratic concept of a programme.

Dividing time

Superficially the youth work programme is akin to a school timetable in that it divides the life of the club, group, project, troop or pack into blocks of time. However, there are a number of distinguishing features separating the two.

First, given that attendance is voluntary, a programme must be constructed around the enthusiasms, interests and concerns of the young people who are involved, or may become so if it is attractive enough, in the life of the youth organisation. As Baden-Powell (1908) stressed, the youth worker must scatter bread on the water to entice the fish. The programme is the bait. Consequently as Spence and Devanney with Noonan explain, 'the ability to think creatively about activities and programmes is therefore an important feature of the youth worker's skill' (2007: 60).

Indeed the composition of a programme is in many respects the point of commencement from which so much youth work originates, a starting point radically at odds with that of the schoolteacher drawing up a timetable.

Second, it must be reflexive for unlike the school or college timetable this is an entity that must, to some degree, be negotiable and responsive. Negotiable because those who construct it can only make intelligent guesses as to what may or may not prove appealing to potential 'members'. If they wish to retain the interest of the young people it must be responsive to their expressed desires and preferences. As Lily Montagu rapidly learnt, her club began to thrive when she allowed the members to shape the programme for 'they knew more about the needs of their fellow members than we did' (1954: 36).

Third, because youth work is primarily built around informal education, rather than formal instruction, it has to allow space for the former. In themselves activities, games and outings have only of limited value for educators – although young people may well have fun taking part. Their worth primarily resides in the degree to which they create openings for educational dialogue, for reflection and for the building of relationships. That is, they draw in young people and provide the opportunities for the young people to engage with the youth worker and each other. The school timetable seeks to eradicate as much as possible of the time spent outside the classroom. Unsupervised minutes, necessary for the pupils to visit the toilet or consume their victuals, are kept to the minimum for it is in those instances the influence of the teacher is at its weakest and can easily be supplanted by that of peer groups. Indeed some new academies have gone so far as to eliminate breaks, lunch-hours and playgrounds so young people are denied any opportunity to engage in casual conversation amongst themselves or with teachers during the working day of the school. The youth worker's programme on the other hand is usually designed to maximise the opportunities for groups to form, conversation to take place and relationships to develop.

Fourth, youth work seeks to extend and induct young people into the lived experience of democracy. Within the life of the youth project workers frequently seek to find openings to let democratic decision-making create what Desiree Edwards-Rees (1943: 84) called a 'little commonwealth'. While the school offers a curriculum imposed from outside and restricts student participation (if it occurs at all) to the discussion of trivialities – and sports and leisure-centres provide readymade activity programmes – youth projects and groups are generally able to use the programme as a vehicle for fostering democratic engagement. Indeed the ambition of many youth workers is to achieve what Walker (1943: 109) calls the 'free programme' – whereby the formation and management of the programme is placed in the hands of the members. In other words enabling the 'young people led organisation' to become a reality (Badham and Davies 2007). However, as Robertson reminds us, clubs and projects must be places 'where things happen', therefore, although it may be the 'aim of every worker to get young people in organising the programme' the worker must be prepared to 'help and be a role model' if this is to stand a chance of happening (2005: 66). Whatever may be the level of participation on the part of the young people, the planning of a programme can nevertheless provide a unique starting point for democratic engagement, as well as for teaching the arts of conversation, negotiation and engagement.

Purpose and planning

Programming may be central to much youth work practice; however, the concept is certainly not unproblematic nor is it always clear-cut. Although the terms and language of the debates concerning the nature and content of programmes change over time, two key themes constantly re-emerge. The first of these is the extent to which a programme is managed and structured. Josephine Macalister Brew in her usual trenchant fashion makes it clear where she stands on this issue, vigorously arguing

> There are only two essential guiding principles in programme planning. Neither the programme nor the plan is sacred – a great deal of work amongst adolescents is a process of trial and error and, as we must be prepared to build and plan so we must also be prepared to discard.
>
> (1957: 202)

Others are unhappy with this position. They are concerned that such pragmatism leads to a lack of structure and to a tolerance by workers of the acceptability of 'hanging about'. In particular, the approach advocated by Brew is viewed by some as being especially problematic, even harmful for those most likely to drift into offending and other 'risk behaviours'. Therefore they argue for the 'provision of common objectives, a range of curricula such as sport and music, and engagement in structured youth activities' on the grounds these 'may provide developmental opportunities that can significantly transform their life paths at key transition points' (Feinstein et al. 2006: 324). Indeed this viewpoint has been extended to embrace an element of compulsion with young people being 'obliged' to partake in approved activities for a allocated period of time each week with clubs being vetted to ensure they offer structure and activities and promote regular attendance (Margo et al. 2006).

The second is a demand for what contemporary policy documents such as *Transforming Youth Work* term accredited outcomes, and what past practitioners often called 'pot hunting' or 'badge collecting'. Again Brew addresses this question forthrightly:

> To put it crudely, people who support youth work by their money are seldom willing to support a venture which supplies nothing but what they like to call 'mere amusement'. Therefore the unfortunate leader is too often in the unenviable position of being forced to embark on a programme which shall satisfy the desire for uplift demanded by the subscribers to the club, and at the same time to cater for the club member who is not ready for this uplift and resists it to the last gasp. It is this Puritanical conception, that if people are enjoying themselves they are probably not learning anything which is at the root of much of the acknowledged dishonesty behind many annual reports.
>
> (1949: 43)

Nowadays we might add the dishonesty behind many evaluations and 'awards' of dubious worth given to young people. Many such 'awards' being carefully crafted to attach spurious evidence of learning to almost every activity or encounter that takes place within the state-funded youth work sector.

The tensions fuelling these debates will never be eradicated. For they reflect profound differences concerning what is, and what is not, an educational experience and what is, and is not, youth work, just as they mirror the enduring friction between work with young people that is driven by a diversionary agenda – keep them off the streets, keep them out of trouble – and work motivated by an educational one. For the former the prime aim of the programme is to occupy and divert, therefore unearthing a formula that is 'popular', irrespective of whether it is demanding or educationally meaningful, becomes the prime role of the worker. By way of contrast the educational model can produce its own tensions. For example, much 'educational' youth work is now formulated to 'deliver' externally assembled curricular packages which the youth group or organisation is contracted by an outside agency to dispense. These may be aimed at reducing crime, drug and alcohol usage, obesity and teenage pregnancy or increasing self-esteem, self-respect and educational performance. 'Delivering' such materials can be highly problematic and the evidence that youth workers are more successful at doing so than schoolteachers, or that youth clubs are better venues for their dissemination than school classrooms is not conclusive (Hirsch 2005). What is not debatable is that their growing presence within programmes reflects a shift away from informal towards formal education and erodes the time and space that can be devoted to negotiated activities and self-education.

For youth work driven by an educational purpose, rather than diversionary agenda, the programme must capture the imagination of young people while leaving substantive space for informal education and the fostering of opportunities for democratic engagement. Programmes are a tool, they are a primary way in which the substance of youth work is laid out, but it is not the content. That resides in the dialogue and conversations occurring within and around the programme units.

Putting it all together

There are many factors that should influence the planning of a programme and which impact on whether it is successful both for the organisation and for those it seeks to reach. When we start to develop a project or a piece of youth work we should commence with a clear view as to our aims and what it is we hope to achieve. To get there we need a structure for our work and this is why we use a programme. Often this is negotiated, sometimes it is inflicted upon us by a funder and most of the time it is created through trial and error. In order to create a good programme we need to think of the interests and circumstances of the young people with whom we want to work, or whom we wish to attract or target. Young people may be included in the planning and therefore through negotiation shape the programme, but this is unusual given the ways in which funding and resources are currently allocated. Activities and content, though, can still emerge from the desires and intimidations of the members themselves, as long as we, the workers, are astute enough to offer opportunities for them to become involved and are willing to follow their lead. However informally we do this we should not forget our role as educators or underestimate the intelligence of young people. But there are other things that need to be taken into account. Four elements in particular will now be considered in detail.

What is happening within school and college. The raising of the school-leaving and shrinkage of the youth labour market mean that whereas once the bulk of those affiliated to youth organisations were in employment now the overwhelming majority are in full-time education. This means youth workers must pay careful attention to what those institutions offer young people. With the school curriculum placing ever greater emphasis on the mechanics of numeracy and literacy – and both the school and college focusing on skills that supposedly enhance employability – much that is educationally worthwhile is being jettisoned by the formal sector. Creative subjects such as art and music are marginalised, or worse taught merely as a basket of skills linked to employment, and cultural subjects such as history are no longer compulsory post-14. Consequently fewer young people are able to enjoy a range of artistic, cultural and sporting subjects – activities that once occupied substantive portions of the school timetable. Increasingly educational institutions teach to the National Curriculum and exam syllabi ignoring anything that will not improve their league table positions – as a museum-based community education worker found who organised an event celebrating the life and work of local suffragettes. Not one school turned up to her highly publicised and exciting exhibition. The reason being, she subsequently discovered, that it was not on the curriculum that term so teachers could either not justify or had no interest in finding the time to visit. Also the erosion of catchment areas, the rise of specialist schools and the overall decline in the numbers of young people all mean pupils and students commute far greater distances to school or college. When this is set besides changes in teacher contracts it is not difficult to understand why in recent years there has been a sharp decline in the number and range of after-school clubs and activities being offered. Overall each of these changes can provide opportunities for youth workers to enlarge the scope of their programmes to look beyond the historic standbys of pool, table tennis, five-a-side and the occasional art and craft.

Economic, cultural and social background of the area. It may seem obvious but programme planning has to take account of the location and catchment area a project serves. For example, some projects and groups serve specific geographic areas; increasingly this means in our polarised society the project will be catering for young people of a specific social class or ethnic grouping. Consequently what the programme contains must avoid alienating potential participants before they have crossed the threshold while seeking, over time, to expand the horizons of those who do. It is a difficult balance to achieve. Housing, transport and education policies have each in recent years either encouraged or colluded with those social trends that have generated heightened social and economic polarisation (Power and Tunstall 1995; Dorling et al. 2007; Hanley 2007). As a result much youth work, often unconsciously, is socially divisive, reinforcing rather than eroding difference. In particular, it is rare for projects to cross class divides (Coles et al. 1998). Programmes need to address such macro social issues, albeit without adopting a 'holier than thou' attitude. Opportunities need to be created for encouraging young people not merely to flavour the unusual and unexpected, but also to encounter those who otherwise they might only perceive as being 'different' or 'threatening'. Programmes should strive to involve a wide section of young people in order that they may contribute to their mutual growth through learning about each other and considering themselves a part of society as opposed to being apart from it. However, it is naive to imagine in a society where adult leisure activities overwhelmingly serve to reinforce social segregation, rather than erode it, that youth work can make more than a small impact on this.

Type of young people one wishes to attract and retain. This may seem contradictory given the previous point but workers when developing a programme must have a clear idea of the characteristics, and interests, of the young people they are seeking to attract and keep affiliated to a project or centre. No programme will meet the needs of more than a segment of a given youth population. It is foolish to imagine otherwise. Even the school- or college-based worker must recognise that young people are divided by class, gender and religion in ways that will often lead to an activity or project becoming dominated by one grouping rather than another. Equally young people who opt to affiliate to specific subcultural groupings tend not to contentedly mix one with the other. Types of music, activities and structures all function to both attract and repel young people; this is unavoidable and workers should not be uncomfortable with this reality. Therefore hard choices arise regarding, first, who should be prioritised, and, second, how can some of the barriers, artificial or otherwise, be wholly or partially addressed.

Resources. Once every allowance has been made for the creativity and determination of a team of youth workers to develop a broad, rich and attractive programme, it is inevitable that what is offered will be constrained by access to resources. Availability of resources impacts equally on centres and projects big and small; it always has and always will. At both ends of the continuum, resources partially determine the style, ethos and content of a programme shaping what young people can and will ask for as well as what staff can realistically lay on the table for discussion.

Once all these factors have been taken into account, the task remains of how to create a balanced programme. Riley (2001), in a helpful article, suggests youth workers need to focus on and balance:

- *Short-term activities* that enable workers to get to know young people, will appeal to significant numbers and allow workers the opportunity to address such 'issues' as responsible modes of behaviour and sensitivity to the needs of others;
- *Medium-term projects* such as monthly trips, discos and activities requiring specialist staff. These provide opportunities for young people to be involved in planning and preparation with appropriate support and guidance;

● *Long-term projects* that can include peer education programmes, drama productions, annual camps and residentials. These gift opportunities for sustained engagement between the young people and the workers as well as extensive openings for the former to undertake leadership and organisational roles.

Achieving an equilibrium between each of the above is as important within the context of a one-night-a-week club meeting in a church or village hall as in a purpose-built youth centre or wing open everyday. However, getting the balance right is never easy, whatever the setting. In part because what works this year may seen outmoded and old hat next month. Consequently clubs and youth projects have ups and downs. Needs change, as can tastes, and therefore programmes must be constantly evaluated, critiqued and tinkered with. Perhaps the only rule to be heeded is that workers must avoid the trap of allowing the programme to become a fixed entity to be adhered to until the bitter end.

Planning and programming

For youth workers operating in centres, schools and colleges much of their practice amounts to a drawing together of a series of 'programmes'. Each is a part of a bigger programme that sets out what they will be offering over a year, month or week. One worker, based in a further education college, divided up her time in a programmatic way. Specific times were set for being around – in her office, in the canteen, walking the corridors or hanging out with the smokers congregating by the wheelie bins – so young people knew where to find her if they wished to talk, seek advice, information and help. Other segments of her time were allocated to discrete activities such as the DJ or drama workshops which had prepared programmes and time slots that young people 'signed-up' to. A third part of her wider 'programme' was allotted to developing work with 'excluded' groups within the college community including asylum seekers, refugees and overseas students away from their homeland for the first time.

For this work to be effective careful attention had to be paid to short-, medium- and long-term goals. So, for example, in the short term it was vital to meet and greet students, at whatever time in the college year they arrived, to ensure they were made aware of what support services and help was available. In the medium term they needed to be offered the opportunity to make friends and contacts, to 'settle in' and better understand the nuances of the culture they were entering. The way in which this was approached provides an example of how careful preparation and flexibility can co-exist in relation to programme planning and implementation.

A group of young British-born students, who had been in regular contact with the worker for a year, volunteered to set up a conversation group for peers whose first language was not English. Their aim, shared by the worker, was to help the overseas students 'practise' conversational English and provide a space where friendships could be formed. For the youth worker involved, a number of secondary aims existed including to help the volunteers to learn how to teach informally; develop their own language competency; acquire inter-personal skills; and secure a better understanding of other cultures and life experiences. To enable all this to occur, the worker needed to create a programme that would be attractive to the overseas students, sustain the interest of the volunteers and address the wider educational ends that she sought to meet. A series of meetings, which were held before the new term started, between the volunteers and worker enabled a programme of events and activities to be formulated and subsequently advertised via leaflets and word-of-mouth within the college. It was hoped this would attract additional volunteers and participants. The group designed a programme they hoped would look purposeful and enjoyable. Therefore the initial sessions were an eclectic mix of games and 'ice-breakers' calculated to help the group gel, members to learn something about each other and provide opportunities for conversation and discussion. The focus was on informality and activity. Meetings went well and volunteers took responsibility for planning individual sessions which meant coming prepared with the equipment for a specific activity and thought through ideas for topics.

However, by session four the group decided there was a need for some activities that would get them out and about. A couple of volunteers suggested when they next met if the weather was good they should 'walk along the river' looking at the bridges and talk about their history, design and changing roles. This was enthusiastically agreed and the two who made the suggestion agreed to come with some information on the 'waterfront' and bridges. Fine weather meant the next session became a walk. Henceforth, although elements of the initial programme remained fixed – for example, Bonfire Night, Remembrance Day and a Christmas Party – far greater flexibility became the norm and it was commonplace for volunteers and overseas students alike to suggest activities for following or subsequent meetings. This meant new volunteers and overseas students could join and feel free within a couple of sessions to make 'suggestions'. A combination of planning and improvisation allowed the 20 or so members of the group to produce a varied and responsive programme comprising a mix of conversation, topics, activities, dance, walks, cooking and 'outings'. This programmatic structure allowed new members to be accommodated and fresh ideas tested out – evaluated – for possible inclusion in future programmes.

Having a programme encouraged people to suggest ideas, to offer to bring things. It also meant volunteers knew what was happening in advance and cut out the need to have weekly planning meetings that they had neither the time nor the inclination to attend. What evolved – and not without problems – was a balanced programme that took into consideration the needs of both groups and the restrictions of the environment (e.g., in the first year the base was re-allocated twice). Balancing availability of students and volunteers was an ongoing problem but the students' enthusiasm kept this group going from year-to-year despite annual personnel changes. Often the group moves away from the designated topic but the flexibility of the staff and volunteers ensures the programme is not a straightjacket, but a framework for relationships to form and conversation to take place.

In conclusion

There are different ways of devising a programme. It can be imposed from above by the funding, or workers can find themselves expected to devise the year's programme by consulting the young people involved. This, again, can be handled in alternative ways but can be problematic. For example, one local authority naively expected workers to devise with the young people they were working with a programme of activities for the year. No parameters were given and it was left to the workers to suggest what costs and resources would have to be taken into consideration. Ideas from young people ranged from visits to the ice rink, residentials and visits abroad. As far as the authority's managers were concerned, the important thing was the process of involving young people, the taking account of their ideas and the consultation – included in the setting of the programme. However, this is where it began and ended. Once the consultation was finished and their plans submitted, nothing else happened – the process ended and the devised programme given scant attention due to a lack of funding and shortages of specialist workers. Expectations raised were then dashed, and this confirmed in the minds of some of the participants that young people are neither listened to nor taken seriously.

But there is also another point here. Our job as workers is to raise people's awareness of themselves and the world – to educate in the broadest sense. Therefore by only working with what the young people want they would miss out on what we know to be worthwhile, and the new experiences that open up new horizons. A negotiated programme should be just that, a dialogue between worker and young people. It should also be realistic with young people given information on all the boundaries imposed by funding and restricted resources.

Good programmes link the needs of the young to the enthusiasms and skills of the workers. However, we, as workers, must never get carried away by our enthusiasms. For example, I recall the residential Murder Mystery Weekend – organised down to the last detail by staff who thought it would be a great experience to take the young people on. Every one had a role, every thing was timed, the venue booked and all arranged. The problem was that no one had considered that the young people might not fit in to this organisation, may not want to play the parts allocated to them or would not actually enjoy such an elaborate and complicated game. This was an activity in which an admirable amount of time and thought had been invested but unfortunately the underlying purpose, and the young people themselves, was forgotten. The idea had great potential and with a little more flexibility and involvement by the young people might have been a great success.

Likewise it is vital to ask if what is being offered within the programme is worthwhile or effective. For example, the regular Healthy Eating session organised over a number of years outwardly looked to be a success. In one way it was working very well. The team of workers running the sessions had them operating smoothly – the buying of the food, the setting of the menu or the involvement of young people were all outwardly 'successful'. However, while the young people could prepare the food and were able to talk about the benefits of eating it, as soon as they were finished instead of eating it they immediately went out to the local 'chippy' and bought their usual diet of chips and pasty which they brought back to the project to eat. While they had learnt about healthy eating no way were they actually going to eat the stuff. The manager pulled the plug on the session against fierce opposition from the workers involved who had got so attached to the mechanics of the session and to the weekly routine that they'd lost sight of the purpose. It was not working and better ways needed to be found that engaged the young people but which offered a purposeful outcome.

There is no off-the-shelf formula for constructing a successful programme. Care and attention to detail are vital, as is a willingness to constantly ask if what we are offering coincides with our aims as a centre or project. If it does not coincide then it probably has no place. Even the most experienced worker will include elements that fail. Too little programming and young people don't know what we offer; too much and we become inflexible and leave no room for spontaneity or for involvement in self-education. However, if we seek to ensure the content and activities grow out of the desires and needs of the young people we are over time unlikely to go far wrong.

7 | Activities in youth work

Sean Harte

> Building on the previous chapter this contribution examines the
> place and value of activities within the youth work programme.
> Sean Harte examines their role and function as well as the ways
> in which youth workers can effectively employ activities to achieve
> educational ends.

Activities and activity-based interventions have always loomed large
within youth work practice. However, understanding the theoretical principles and the educational potential underpinning this method of work
has been somewhat limited. This deficiency can be attributed to several factors, including the lack of good quality training and educational
opportunities open to part-time and voluntary youth workers. Also the
inconsistent application of the term youth work which has been used
to describe a plethora of diverse tasks and roles does not help. Similarly, the vague and dissimilar value base of workers in fields of work
with young people, rather than compelling a healthy discourse on different approaches and methodologies around the value or otherwise of
activity work, has minimised the theoretical knowledge base enabling the
common-sense view of 'character building' to proliferate with little serious scrutiny (Taylor 1987). Nevertheless, the importance and meaning
of activities within a wider educational focus must not be neglected in
favour of merely *doing* them, if full advantage is to be gained from their
application.

Activities within youth work generally take on a more specialised
meaning than their everyday usage elsewhere. Within this context 'activities' are a means of engaging with young people whereby workers use

a planned and meaningful focus in order to promote exchange, discourse, challenge and development of the self and others. It is often contrasted with conversation, 'hanging-out' and spontaneous actions. From the perspective of informal educators there are significant dangers in this. Many years ago Don Feasey (1972: 22) made the case for stretching our understanding of activities within youth work to include 'transitory, informal moments'. He argued that we need to accept 'the "one-off", fragmentary experience as of value and frequently a setting for something worthwhile to happen'. 'After all', he continued, 'impulse can express spontaneity and this may lead to innovation.' This said, though, there is a strong argument for attending to the contribution of more formally planned 'activities' in terms of deepening and extending learning, and opening up new opportunities (see, for example, Mahoney *et al.* 2005).

Planning is crucial to ensure suitability, relevance and challenge. Within most contexts it is also essential for staff to ensure the activity does not endanger the safety and well-being of participants. With the growth of the 'where there's blame, there's a claim' culture, young people's physical safety has repeatedly come under the microscope for critical analysis. Risk assessment should, of course, be an integral component of any activity-based work in order to take precautions and consider remedial emergency actions as required to prevent injury or even death. However, current trends in policy and practice have drawn us closer to risk eradication rather than minimisation to controlled levels (Furedi 2001, 2005). This can, and often does, impinge on the potential for education and learning. However, that debate is not the focus for this discussion. While risk assessment for physical danger is now commonplace for activities, less understood or considered is the potential emotional significance which may be exposed during participation. While undertaking and achieving some degree of success in a new and challenging activity may indeed build confidence and self-esteem, what consideration is given to the longer-term impact of not overcoming one's fears within the public group environment of many activities? For example, a young girl who became very upset and afraid to abseil during a residential I attended was re-assured and supported at the time, but what thought and theory had considered her short- and longer-term emotional well-being prior to the event?

To a confident experienced worker the planning of an activity need not be a complicated or prolonged undertaking. Yet it is necessary to make explicit the need for effective planning within activity-based work and allow adequate time for it to take place. Participation in activities offers potential, nothing more. It is the worker's role to enable participants to harness this potential, to secure opportunities to learn, change and grow. This requires skilful employment of evaluative processes and a sound underpinning knowledge base.

A starting point

Activities are an excellent starting point for youth work (Mahoney *et al.* 2005). First, they provide the worker with an opportunity to engage with groups and individuals they might not otherwise reach. For example, the interest of a group of young Asian males in cricket, while potentially reinforcing stereotypes, could enable a white-dominated youth provision to plan and develop an activity programme to engage this group, widen participation and over time expand the provision to consider diversity and challenge inequalities. Second, activities provide a chance to start work at a point where the young people *are*.

> Initially, young people may be attracted by the opportunity to take part in activities. They may decide to go along with things to see what they can get out of it for themselves – grasping the chance for a free weekend away or involvement in activities like 'canoeing camping or whatever'. Pretty soon, however, they realise that there is more to this youth work than they first thought. They acquire and develop new skills and abilities. They look inside themselves and ask 'what am I doing here?' and 'where do I want to progress to in my life?'
>
> (Young 2006: 65)

Activities may be used as an attraction to encourage engagement, but ultimately they are far more powerful (Brew 1957; Foreman 1987). Meaningful engagement in activities can provide young people with the means to become *who they are* or more importantly the chance to become or fully understand *who they want to be*. Here the educational role of the worker should not be underestimated. Many young people's early life experiences have drawn them to develop unrealistic, low or socially undesirable aspirations. While this is challenging for both worker and young person, it is exactly this challenge which can be the foundation for effective informal education, enabling new knowledge to be considered and embraced by both parties as a consequence of the dialogical analysis of their experiences, values, perceptions and beliefs.

Activities can clearly range from participation in simple short tasks such as a game of Pictionary to more complex mechanisms such as planning and organising a democratic process for project representatives to sit on the management committee. Both of these can be effectively utilised by youth workers. Equally they demand of the worker a degree of thought and planning. Careful consideration needs to be given to possible unintended as well as the intended outcomes and aims. Workers will have to choose between alternatives and reflect upon what activity among many may secure the most desirable process and outcome. Indeed, some activities may well be rejected as totally unacceptable as they are incompatible with the philosophy of youth work existing within the project, or at odds with the aims of the work. This topic in itself requires greater exploration than can be achieved here; however, if we are clear about the educational aims of our work we must consider any potential activity within this context, for even an innocuous-seeming activity can act to reinforce views and attitudes that might not approximate to those a worker would seek to encourage.

The world of activities with young people does not simply reflect societal inequalities and social problems; it reproduces and reinforces them unless a specific oppositional stance is taken. For example, a straightforward trip to the zoo is likely to reinforce that it is acceptable to cage wild animals, while a discussion on the pros and cons during or after the same trip would enable participants to form personal opinions. Similarly, a simple un-moderated group discussion on views of sex and relationships can quickly move to promoting the majority view. As educators we need to think about giving a fair amount of weighting to alternatives in order to encourage people to reflect and come to more considered understandings. We have to appreciate the complexities of even the simplest activity and ask questions of it. For example, if an activity to explore homophobic views is likely to reinforce current opinion because of the group's developmental stage or personal opinions, does that render the activity inappropriate or not?

Some activities may be placed out-of-bounds by a funder or employing agency if they are at odds with their dominant values. For some workers within a school, empowering activities highlighting issues of inequality within the formal education system would be taboo. Activities supporting sex and relationship education are heavily censored in some schools and organisations because of the pervading religious beliefs, and in some culture-specific organisations mixed-sex activities are not permitted. Even where such activities are allowed, this can lead to conflict with colleagues or managers. For example, a project around understanding parenthood, including the positive personal and social aspects this can develop, was deemed to be promoting the benefits of teenage pregnancy and this landed the worker in hot water. Therefore, there are many factors impinging on the range and scope of activities at a worker's disposal prior to beginning to plan a programme.

Workers should, wherever possible, make every attempt to involve participants within the planning process. Indeed, the best activity ideas are frequently those contrived by young people themselves. The most successful disco in terms of attendance and enjoyment I have seen was planned entirely by a group of young people wishing to organise a special event for a member of staff leaving the project. From haggling over disco costs to organising refreshments, printing tickets and drumming up custom and interest among their peers the group achieved something in excess of what the staff could have expected. Yes, many of the skills employed in planning and organising the event were developed through earlier work, as was the confidence to take control of this event, but the fact remains this activity was such a success because it was led by young people.

Many activities will last a full day such as planning, discussing, researching and acting out a mock trial to explore the concepts of justice and fairness and how these are applied within the British legal system. Some activities cannot even be attempted in anything less; however, the structure and nature of youth work means most will have to be condensed into a session of an hour or two, or occasionally less perhaps a few minutes. While young people's participation in such an activity may indeed last only 30 minutes or less, the whole activity process – that is, the planning, doing and learning – is likely to go well beyond this timeframe. For example, a group activity designed to explore participant's abilities to work as part of a team could be completed in 30 minutes to an hour; but in order to be effective a worker must have planned the activity, taking account of likely participant's skills and the prospective pitfalls. Upon completion much potential exists for participants to have learned about themselves and this might be achieved over a lengthy period by using the activity as a reference point to look back upon. Projects have continuity over a prolonged period of time, ranging from a couple of weeks to several months, or years. Here we begin to touch upon the transcendence of activities into project working. Projects are more than a series of inter-linked activities; they show development and progression to participants evidencing significant movement and change or development of understanding between beginning and end. Activities will vary in duration but tend to be on short time scales as opposed to lengthier project-based work.

In summary an effective youth work activity needs to take account of group and individual well-being, the processes involved in providing it and the likely outcomes, desired or otherwise, that may result. While these may not always be given equal importance and weighting, the balancing of these factors does become a key point for ensuring that a cohesive learning environment is maintained and that the educational potential of an activity is exploited.

Education and learning through activities

Activities are tools. They provide a key setting to enable the educational processes of youth work to take place. They act as a catalyst to initiate and hasten young people's development and learning. Activities, as part of a co-ordinated programme (see previous chapter by Gilchrist on this topic), are an excellent starting point for work with young people. They provide an initial attraction for young people to become engaged, perhaps to try something new and exciting or to show off existing talents.

Activities assist in the process of relationship building, especially where worker and young person participate together, with both learning side-by-side, for example, on a first aid or food hygiene course. This experience of mutual education reflects a worker's acceptance that they are not the fountain of all knowledge, that they are still seeking to learn and that they value education for themselves not merely others. Thus, the two become equals in the learning process undertaken and this position can then be reinforced during future conversations, discussions and activities. Within the context of shared participation the more traditional adult – young person relationship, with all the imbalances of power favouring the adult that are embodied within it, can be reduced or even set aside. This gives a clearly oppositional stance to the usual pedagogical hierarchy adopted within formal learning or teaching environments. While the positions of teacher and student – in this example – remain, the relationship between worker and young person is re-configured. This shift thereby enables a worker to explore the contextual element of knowledge within formal education and of course highlight the alternative approach taken within informal education.

Certain activities may encourage young people to gain confidence from new experiences and explore personal issues and boundaries. This is a valid reason to attempt many pieces of work but all too often it is used to legitimise a poorly planned activity such as a trip to a leisure park or aqua-centre. Newness is a validating basis only where the newness elucidates potential for learning and furthermore where the worker embraces and embellishes the newness. Without this, repetition and familiarity are likely to inhibit rather than utilise potentiality. Similarly, new experiences which reinforce existing views and prejudices are no better a tool for youth work than any facet of a daily routine. While activities may help young people discover new skills and interests or develop those already existing, in isolation, participation in prescribed one-off or programmed activity, though often beneficial, adheres more to what Foreman (1987) designated the Redcoat style of youth work. Here it is argued that some youth work is more concerned with entertaining young people than fostering their education and social development. Rather than being a starting point and a means to an end, 'Redcoats' allow activities to take over and become an end in themselves; they see the intrinsic value of activities but fail to explore or exploit their potential.

Utilising a broad range of activities will increase the likelihood of sustained interest among members and enable them to encounter fresh, challenging and stimulating experiences. The more varied the programme the better, as this can encourage participants to be creative in suggesting new activity ideas, perhaps even outside of envisaged group norms. It will also expose them to the potential of exploring, discovering and developing new skills, interests and beliefs.

Often it is not an activity itself which enables learning. Participation in an activity sometimes merely offers the time and opportunity to talk and discuss. In this way activities work to facilitate dialogue which may challenge or reinforce existing views and experiences, but only where a worker chooses to make use of this opportunity. Through activities and facilitated dialogue there are possibilities to increase the self-worth of individuals and develop their ability to accept others and value difference. Rosseter's (1987) discussion on the educational philosophy of youth work highlights these outcomes, declaring that participation in activities and projects is, alongside role modelling, problem solving, consciousness raising and critical involvement, one of the five inter-linked methodologies of social and political education. Within a constructive group context this approach allows members further opportunities for growth and development. Participants can see how every individual has worth in their knowledge, skills and value base while also observing that even academic 'high flyers' are not always exceptional at everything. However, although we may not be particularly skilful, adept or outstanding at something we may nevertheless gain enormous satisfaction from engagement with it, be it a solitary or group activity. For the youth worker, as opposed to the coach or trainer, although they may seek to offer young people a route towards securing an interest or affiliation to an activity that may offer long-term satisfactions the prime aim is to cultivate enriching relationships with others. Therefore, the youth work focus has been upon activities that bring people together rather than isolate them. To encourage engagement with and in activities that lead to them valuing shared experiences and that foster a productive group identity (Payne 2005). This can be particularly important and advantageous with targeted work aimed towards socially excluded young people or those displaying anti-social behaviour as it can help to reinforce more acceptable group norms. Indeed, through developing and fostering group participation and identity with young people the often-maligned influence of *peer pressure* can be seen to have a positive value. Generally, we find it is more likely to be beneficial than negative in terms of impact (Rich Harris 1998). Acceptable group norms can generally be far more effective at encouraging changes in behaviour than the continuous pleadings, ranting and raving of a youth worker, teacher, parent or social worker, however well-intentioned these are.

The feelings of worth created from a shared involvement in group activities is not limited to young people exhibiting problem behaviour. Participation can help young people to better understand themselves, how they think and act and why they think and act in the ways they do. This in turn may enable them to locate where, how and why they belong. For instance, exploring the characteristics you would like to see in a 'best friend', and most importantly why, can show young people what values and behaviours are sought in others and why this is so. In a diverse group this may highlight some different views, but it is likely that the majority of desirable characteristics will be present in any group. Following this, participants could be enabled to understand what it is that others like and dislike in their behaviours and thus the activity begins to offer the potential to learn about self and perhaps even harness support to modify any undesirable findings. Through the discovery of new skills and the continuous constructive challenge of perceived self and surroundings that activity work can offer, young people may find the transition from childhood, through adolescence and into adulthood, which all traverse, a more bearable, interesting and fulfiling journey. In a subtle way then, experiences evolved from activities in youth work settings can meet a variety of needs from belonging, esteem and personal adequacy to respect for others and increased social understanding. Their potential for the worker who uses them wisely can be, in many respects, limitless.

Theories and models in activities – how does it happen?

The educational value in activities primarily resides in the experience or experiences that can be gained from participation. Basically experiences within youth work can be placed upon a recreation/education continuum, with activities ranging from the unalloyed pursuit of fun to a fulfiling educational experience or anywhere in between. This of course is not to imply that educational experiences cannot and should not be fun for participants. When the element of fun is retained the educational rewards can be seen to proliferate. Through harnessing enjoyment workers can often encourage participation in pursuits that may otherwise be overlooked or avoided. For example, some young people's enthusiasm for leisure time reading is often dampened, if not extinguished, by the insistence of schools that they read specific texts according to a pre-determined curriculum. Conversely, a youth work relationship may foster a love of reading by nurturing young people's interests through discussion and questioning and by encouraging them to read what excites them. The differentiation to be made is that an activity that *is* fun is very different to one that is *for* fun. It is only with the benefit of a sound theoretical knowledge base and some degree of experience that this difference can be clearly identified. Indeed, most activities can be placed at either end of this continuum or somewhere in between.

Recreation ⟵——————————⟶ Education

Activity

It is the skills or lack of them, employed by the worker, which differentiates its position and often this difference would not be apparent to the casual observer (for an excellent discussion of this issue, see Hirsch 2005).

Throughout their lives each individual will be part of countless experiences, yet not all promote the growth and changes that would allow us to categorise them as educational. What then is it that sets some experiences apart from others and defines them as, or enables them to be, educational processes? One determining factor for differentiating these experiences is the ability to assess and comprehend these experiences within an individual and societal context. That is, to understand what has been gained from an experience, to grasp the possibilities that were not open previously and acquire a personal frame of reference around which to interpret the meaning of that encounter. It is within this capacity for understanding that the primary function of the youth worker as a facilitator of activities becomes distinct.

As noted earlier activities and thus experiences are not necessarily intrinsically educational, although many do posses this inherent potential. The key to learning through experience lies not only in the quality of experience which is to be had, but in the ability to reflect upon, deconstruct, internalise and use the experience to promote growth. In short, the evaluation of the experience is, in the youth work context, often the most significant contribution towards the learning of all the parties. The point at which, as Myles Horton explains, it 'becomes possible to draw out of people their experiences' (1990: 57).

Evaluating activities

With heightened theoretical understanding and grasp of the key methodologies evaluative exercises and debriefing techniques can be harnessed by youth workers to much greater effect. However, without the theoretical knowledge with which to frame these experiences any evaluation or debriefing is of limited value. It is lamentable that youth work, as a profession, has not made explicit the far-reaching consequences of improved learning for young people that can be obtained from thorough and effective evaluation of activities undertaken with participants through structured debriefing. In order to achieve this sufficient time must be allowed, remembering that as an educational medium without evaluation the activity remains unfulfiled. Workers should be skilled in questioning techniques and language use in order to elucidate not just *what* occurred but *why* it occurred and what thought processes were employed during this time. Furthermore, to support learning, discussion should not be confined to the past and what happened but should explore the future and possibilities which are now open due to learning from an activity. For example, what happens regularly that has parallel with what has been observed? Learning from what was discussed how might this now be viewed or handled differently?

Such evaluation undertaken with young people has long been high on the agenda. Consequently a plethora of agencies involved in working with young people are obliged, as a condition attached to the receipt of funding, to extend the participation and involvement of young people or users in evaluating practice and re-formulating the focus and delivery of services. However, it does appear that a lack of understanding, and in many cases competence, prevails in making extensive use of the possibilities debriefing and evaluation offer. Often the scope of evaluation is limited to ticking boxes enquiring – 'Did you enjoy the activity, yes or no?' Slightly preferably is the expansion to – 'What did you enjoy about this activity? What didn't go well? How could it be improved?' Alas, all too frequently, evaluation is neglected entirely and while initiatives such as *Transforming Youth Work* (DfES 2002) and *Aiming High for Young People* (HM Treasury 2007) highlight the need for evaluative methods, regrettably it is often viewed as a paper exercise undertaken to placate management. Some workers, full- and part-time, do not see it as an intrinsic part of activity-based work. Others fail to differentiate between evaluation with young people, in order to enhance the learning opportunities created by participation and involvement, and professional evaluation or reflection, in order to improve the worth of future activities, thereby blurring the two or neglecting one entirely. As described the real value of experience as an educational instrument lies with the participant. While a skilled worker may support or even ensure learning takes place the impact of this remains internal to the participant. Thus evaluation with participants helps close the loop of learning (Kolb 1984). Reflective evaluation is more concerned with the development of professional practice. Here a worker considers the efficacy of activities chosen and their application and how this may be developed in order to improve the quality of the next experience (Schön 1987). While participant's views here are important they are not strictly central to this evaluative process.

Time and resources would be well employed improving understanding of the critical importance of evaluation within experiential learning. Helpfully Dewey explains,

> The greater maturity of experience which should belong to the adult as educator puts him in a position to evaluate each experience of the young in a way which the one having the less mature experience cannot do.
>
> (1963: 38)

This reminds us that the key difference between young people and ourselves is the variation in the range of life experiences acquired over time. While this is inherently true of a younger age group the concept can be equally applied to those in their late teens/early twenties if we consider that the meaning applied to, and derived from, experiences is integral to learning. It is implicit then that workers should be able to draw upon a range of 'quality' life experiences rather than simply assuming greater knowledge through the quantity of experiences encountered by virtue of having lived longer. Without sufficient understanding of the potential role evaluation can play in the learning process and the methods which can be employed, the adult, or youth worker, is in no stronger a position to draw learning from the experience than the participant.

Throughout the history of youth work as an educational process reflection through debriefing can be seen as a central element in assessing the success or failure of activities (Russell 1932; Henriques 1933). A competent and confident worker, trained and skilled in the art of debriefing, should understand the relationship between activity and experience seeing them as integral parts of a single process rather than separate entities. Workers are then positioned to utilise debriefing techniques to engage young people in dialogue and conversation about their experiences, feelings and understandings in relation to an activity, stage or entire project. It is in this debriefing process that the full potential of each experience may be gained. This technique has been harnessed to great effect by the Prince's Trust 'Personal Development Programme'. Upon completion of each activity the team leader conducts a session to discuss what occurred in terms of participation, non-participation, feelings and thought processes. This systemically draws upon learning from earlier activities and debriefs in a way that positively reinforces or challenges current thinking. Over time these sessions encourage participants to reflect upon how they can and will apply this knowledge to their own lives and move towards achieving their ultimate potential. Thus effective debriefing encompasses past, present and future with the activity serving as a conduit to reinforce learning. Ideally, this process is followed by further discussion to assess the impact of this learning some time in the future.

Challenges and issues in activity-based work

Probably the most deep-seated problem of activity- and project-based schemes in contemporary youth work lies within the evaluation of experiences. One cannot measure the quality of experience with a ruler, nor can its value be weighed with scales. Herein lies a perplexing enigma. Dewey, while acknowledging the difficulty of candid qualitative evaluation of experience, guides us to employ the dimension of continuity as a measure. As he argues, 'every experience is a moving force. Its value can be judged only on the ground of what it moves toward and into' (1963: 38). For Dewey a positive educational experience can be differentiated from the less meaningful by analysing the opportunity offered for continuing and sustained learning. In simple terms good experiences open doors, while less inspiring ones are likely to close them. Dewey also relates how learning can be good, or bad such as in the case of a burglar becoming more adept through experience, relating this to the philosophy of sustaining and retarding continuity. However, he never accounts for exactly how this can be gauged leaving it as an open question to be answered by the reader. Here is the crux of the evaluative problem. The worth of any experience lies in the mind of they who judge it, and is thus associated to their value system and beliefs. This renders objective evaluation impossible, though of course we all still attempt it.

So who judges the quality of experiences offered within youth work activities and whose values pervade: youth workers, managers, organisations or government? To some extent, all of the above and this is where individual and organisational discrepancies may become explicit thereby breeding professional anxiety and tension. Ultimately the value of any experience is only likely to be accurately gauged by the individual who has had it. However such a judgement frequently alters over time. Thus last week's party, which was so exciting and socially important, fades to insignificance, while the visit to grandfather the week before, so resented at the time, may come to acquire a profound magnitude as the years pass. Equally the same experience may impact upon the members of a group in unpredictable and divergent ways. The overwhelming majority may deem the hour wasted. One or two might now or later judge it to have been thought-provoking or inspirational. All this indicates that a meaningful evaluation of *activities* is difficult to achieve, especially where dialogue is in itself the activity, as this challenges the narrow stereotyped view of activity often observed and is problematic to evaluate from a positivist position with reference to measured outcomes.

The true focus for qualitative evaluation needs to be upon the experience of the participants; therefore, what the worker records will often be of secondary importance. Once we acknowledge this we begin to highlight flaws in the mechanisms often employed as evaluative tools. Ticking boxes and quoting curriculum areas covered is straightforward but fails to ensure the value of learning is captured. If learning is subjective then this should be acknowledged and participants should be central. Learning can be evidenced via conversation and dialogue in revisiting experiences and exploring knowledge. This evaluative process is of more value to participants as it reinforces learning through questions such as 'do you remember when . . .', 'what happened when . . .', 'why did this happen?', 'how can this be used?' and 'what effects might this have?'. Such questions cannot easily be encapsulated into an evaluation form and even if they were would become less significant. If evidence is required of learning outcomes perhaps, for example, video or audio recordings of these dialogues would be more suitable for this purpose.

Dangers and risks

There are inherent dangers in using 'successful' or popular activities to attract young people into the youth work setting. Often those most widely held to be good for this purpose fit into a narrow paradigm and, moreover, attract a partial and restricted range of youngsters, though this can be advantageous to draw in specific target groups. One recently popular attendance booster with young people is the use of record decks to engage in (or spectate on) MC'ing and the like. This can generate a substantial increase in the 'reach' figure being achieved, but the vast majority of these attendees have had little or no interaction with a youth worker, let alone a significant discourse. Moreover, the young people involved tend to be relatively homogenous as a group, male 14 to 16 and with an interest in a particular kind of music.

As a consequence of this shift many supposedly 'generic' projects end up predominately catering for young males of a certain kind. This often creates a homogenous atmosphere but it is of 'exclusion' rather than 'openness' and may even go as far as deterring some young people you are aiming to attract. Moving activities on from this point can be difficult. If a group become cohesive and the norms set within a narrow activity range they may be unwilling to experiment and move outside their comfort zones. Strong groups of this type are often seen engaging in football within the gym every evening with staff complaining that they will not try anything different. A skilled and confident youth worker can not only redress this situation – they can prevent it occurring in the first place.

Similarly, problems may arise where workers only initiate activities that '*fit*', that is, tailoring activities to certain stereotypes and preconceptions about the groups and individuals they are working with. Girls' groups can typically be observed employing such activities as health and beauty or fashion workshops. While these activities can and do encourage participation from this frequently marginalised group, one often wonders how stated aims of redressing inequalities and oppression are achieved through such work. Superior projects use such activities appropriately interspersed with more challenging work to meet their commendable aims; others lacking in theoretical knowledge fail to appreciate this important distinction. Accomplished workers find ways to initiate activities that move beyond young peoples' accepted norms without risking a loss of trust. Narrow activity programmes can become stifling and habitual, making it extremely difficult for workers to 'break the mould' and broaden the horizons of a well-established group. While acknowledging the benefits of activity-based work in terms of personal development and the growth of inter-personal skills, we must not overlook the real dangers of allowing stereotypes to flourish and the safe and predictable to be replicated *ad nauseum*.

A fundamental problem associated with activity-based work is that of focus. As discussed earlier activity has the potential to be a worthwhile educational tool, but this is not always harnessed. A frequent reason for this is a misapplication of focus. Here emphasis is placed upon the activity as an end in itself rather than a means to an end. This approach is typified by the *buy in* approach, which sees a series of uncoordinated activities and trips offered to young people who opt to *buy in* to those that appeal (or which their friends enjoy). This approach does not require those who partake to contribute to the planning and formulation of the activity, nor are they encouraged to analyse why they are buying into one rather than another endeavour. Such activities may be popular, but often relate more closely to the programme of a leisure centre or social club than the prospectus of an agency committed to educational outcomes.

In youth work, as elsewhere, it is possible to nurture the specialist activity worker. Specialists can make an activity educational, memorable and efficacious. However, there are inherent dangers in employing their services. For specialists often focus on the activity in ways that forgo the learning potential within it. They set aside the needs of the young people in order to focus on the activity. For them the aim is winning the cup, staging the play or climbing the mountain. All very laudable, perhaps, but is it youth work? It is in the nature of the beast that a specialist will, all too often, focus upon participation in and completion of a specific task-based activity and in the process discard the dialogical exchanges and learning opportunities participation in an activity can foster. The youth worker who employs a specialist must be prepared to share an activity in order to exploit these opportunities or set time aside to cultivate reflection.

Specialists, though, do have something to offer beyond a different pitch and an unusual face. Young people all have talents and skills; in many cases these are untapped resources which may never be harnessed. Through the planned introduction of work with specialists in a range of areas such as sport, art or drama young people may gain the opportunity to discover and build skills they would otherwise not have an opportunity to use. There could be a Wimbledon champion in the project who has never used a racquet or at the very least someone who will subsequently take up climbing as a hobby because they did it with the youth club and enjoyed it. After the initial whinges about trying something new die away, most young people will happily give some suggestions as to what to try next, especially if you have helped them gain the confidence to do so.

Sometimes the youth worker has to use every last drop of cunning to enable occasions for informal education to take place, and perhaps the journey to and from a specialist instructor in hair design or beauty therapy can give just that opportunity. In this instance an activity can be a conduit to access young people, perhaps even a specific target group, and the role of the youth worker may predominately be on this occasion to engage with the young people on the minibus during the journey there and back.

In conclusion

The potential of activity-based work to encourage and facilitate learning on a number of levels has been discussed. Exposure to newness, through a fresh activity or one experienced differently, can promote discovery and knowledge of self, others or one's surroundings. Offering a range of activities with clearly considered potential for different types of learning has been and continues to be at the heart of many youth work projects and rightly so.

Through activities young people can experience the world, discover themselves, develop and grow towards their true potential and make considerable changes to their lives. However, merely providing and facilitating activities will achieve little; certainly it will not ensure learning takes place. Without the correct balance of planning, delivering, debriefing and evaluation offering a diet of activities may lead to stagnation and meaningless commotion. We must remember that activity-based learning is a process and in order to best facilitate learning young people must be placed firmly at the centre of that process. When this occurs activities are likely to be done with young people rather than for or to them. Yet although so much effort may be consumed by the planning and organising of activities so often it is the conversation during or more often after an activity that imparts the opportunity for learning.

8 | Advising and mentoring

Gina McLeod

This chapter, drawing in part on research interviews undertaken by Gina McLeod, seeks to explore issues and questions such as when it is appropriate, or not, to be an adviser or mentor and what these processes mean for practitioners and young people alike. Finally, the chapter considers the tensions arising between advising and mentoring.

So much of the work we do with and alongside young people in youth work and informal education can be described as 'advising', 'mentoring', 'guidance', 'advocacy' or 'counselling'. Frequently, we encounter the question or even lament 'Don't know what I want?' when engaging with young people. And regularly youth workers responded with a timely 'So, have you thought about doing . . . ?' This kind of informal dialogue and relationship building between young people and youth workers has not significantly changed over the years. That is because talking about our concerns and worries, looking to responsible others to help us make decisions is an integral component of youth work – for workers and young people alike. What has changed is the way this organic process has become formally recognised and specifically identified in many settings as being 'advice', 'mentoring', 'guidance' or 'counselling'.

Gradually youth work agencies in the United Kingdom have incorporated and recruited individuals who describe themselves as counsellors, careers/personal advisers, life-coaches and mentors rather than youth workers. These have been employed within such diverse settings as schools, youth clubs, community projects, prisons, colleges, churches and religious organisations. They are also being found in specific places established to provide such workers with a base such as Youth Information and Advice Shops. Less common now are the more relaxed and informal environments of adventure playgrounds, generic youth clubs and 'the streets' as places where youth workers engage young people on their own terms. Instead workers increasingly find themselves operating in more formal environments such as schools, further education colleges, prisons and young offender's institutions where they are expected to 'deliver' issue-based programmes and focused interventions.

As a consequence of this shift, major employers now expect and even demand that workers be trained in 'young people skills' such as counselling, advocacy, advising and mentoring. Such skills are valued by many organisations as the preferred way for practitioners to reach out and work with 'clients'. Especially those young people deemed by others to be a problem and/or judged to be either already or at risk of becoming disaffected or socially excluded. Organisations tend to favour these targeted interventions. First because they attract funding, as a consequence of their apparent capacity to address the specific 'needs' of disaffected and 'at risk' young people. Second because they appear to offer identifiable outcomes that enable staff to be more easily monitored and evaluated. Individualised casework and more open-ended mentoring and advice programmes, operating as they do with individuals, can more easily assess 'distance travelled' by means of tests and case notes as well as meticulously record length and regularity of contact (Philip 2008; Rhodes and Lowe 2008).

The changes outlined above make it essential for students and practitioners to have a clear understanding of what advising and mentoring mean within the context of their working environment.

What is advice?

For those involved in youth work and informal education, the term advice will resonate in different ways. The human experience affords us both personal and professional encounters and opportunities for giving as well as receiving advice. Some will be welcomed and some not – a reality workers need to keep constantly in the forefront of their minds. Unwelcome, unsolicited, advice is often resented: just as much when it emanates from 'qualified' youth workers as when it is proffered by parents, teachers or peers. Individuals of course can actively seek out advice from others. Although whether they then decide to act upon it usually remains a personal and individual choice. Fine, but, what does this mean for us in a professional sense? What are the implications of giving advice to young people within a professional youth work context? And, what do we actually understand by the term advice?

Young people usually have a clear idea of what advice encompasses. As one explained to me, it is 'helping a friend out when they're feeling kind of confused or stressed – y' know, just taking time out to listen and being there for them' (Alicia, aged 16). Another defined it as 'being able to be honest to your friends, like when they're talking about girls and stuff, you have to tell them what it's about without lying to them, that's proper advice' (Raj, aged 15). A third provided a warning as to the care that must be taken by those proffering it.

Advice can sometimes be dangerous cos I had a careers advisor at school who told me that I was wasting my time trying to be a top chef. If it weren't for my Dad's back up I wouldn't have bothered going to catering college, instead, I would be messing about in 6th Form.

(David, aged 17)

Like people of all ages these examples show how individuals both select the source from which they seek advice and evaluate what is offered. In other words it is never a one-way process.

Place of advice within youth work

Advice giving is a process whereby a person (the advisor) generally offers up some kind of 'help' to another (the advisee). Depending on the situation this 'help' may take the form of opinions, suggestions, recommendations or support, and frequently it may incorporate a sharing of life experiences. For example, often the giver may compare the situation being encountered by the young person with a similar one they lived through at the same point in their lives. Indeed, the centrality of this approach to much practice encourages some to argue that it is important to select staff on the basis of similarity of background to those they work with. However, such an approach is not always appropriate because, and the case is often somewhat simplistically put, neither wisdom nor empathy automatically flows from experiences encountered. Indeed, it can produce a tendency towards rigidity – 'this is how I successfully managed so why can't you?' Personal experience has an important role to play, but so does knowledge of other people's along with insights gleaned from literature, films and other cultural material.

Within a professional youth work setting the advice process takes on a distinct and meaningful dimension. It is significantly different from advice given over the telephone to a friend or in a snatched conversation after work. First because youth work is essentially about building and developing relationships through trust and mutuality. Therefore, it is implied by the nature of the relationship that the worker will treat any information given as being confidential and that the advice presented will be in the best interests of the young person rather than those of the worker. Second youth workers should be seeking at all times to be working alongside young people in ways that are authentic, ethical and developmental. Third the youth worker must take more care than the 'person in the street' when engaging in advice-giving. For negative and damaging advice must be avoided at all costs because the interests of the young person will, in most cases, be paramount and because the reputation of the worker and project relies on the quality of the advice given. Ill-thought-out and inappropriate opinions may not merely disadvantage the recipient but discourage others from seeking advice in the future both from the individual concerned and possibly from other youth workers.

Where workers are genuinely young person-centred the advice process can often be useful and beneficial. For example, when a young woman I had been working alongside for some time asked me for some 'help' with her 'family problems'. Briefly, she wanted to know how to put herself into 'care' as she no longer wanted to live at home with Mum. In terms of any help or advice offered, I felt it was important to keep it real and explore with her what she wanted to achieve. By this, I meant explaining to her with blunt honesty the rigmaroles of the English statutory care system along with discussing other possibilities such as foster carers and families. By drawing upon knowledge plus personal experience I was able to engage in a meaningful conversation around the issue of her 'family problems' as well as discussing possible ways forward. Regardless of any advice proffered I had ultimately to respect the choices she would eventually make. In this particular situation, the young woman struggled to resolve her predicament there and then for obvious reasons. She made use of the opportunity to talk things through confidentially and decided that she would try and 'sort things out' in the meantime until she was in a position to live independently. Advice in this context was essentially a mix of knowledge and shared personal experience sought from a person she trusted. In this context I felt advice should avoid being directive. That is, the advisor should refrain from suggesting to an advisee 'you should do this . . . ' or 'if I were you I would do this' – far better to offer information, alternatives and assistance in helping them to clarify what they sought to accomplish.

Advice giving is an activity or process that frequently involves only two parties; however, this is not always the case. Partly because several young people may seek advice simultaneously or because the one who wants the advice is too nervous or unsure to approach the worker alone and consequently brings a friend for support. Often this will be helpful and offer an opportunity for the youth worker to engage in dialogue that focuses on the 'problem' and encourage the members of the group to be mutually supportive. However, at times it has to be recognised that this may not always be achievable. That for some members of the group the problem may be an 'entertainment' while being far more serious for others. Likewise, problems of confidentiality are heightened in group settings and therefore considerable skill and expertise may be required on the part of the worker when working with groups in this context. Workers should not be passive with regard to this area of their practice. Careful analysis of the young people one is working with, plus a deep knowledge of the community in which they live, is essential if we are to avoid giving inappropriate advice. Watching and listening, reading the world around them are as always vital skills for effective youth work. The data accumulating from these activities will lead a worker to be able to better predict what they are likely to be asked and to better prepare to respond effectively. Whatever the setting, sensitivity is essential both to avoid undermining the impact of the message or to avoid alienating the young people who are often 'sick of being told what is best for them'. All this requires forethought and expertise. For example, knowledge that stolen goods are being sold to club members means a worker will not be taken by surprise when asked 'what should I do about this?' by a member. Equally, such knowledge will enable a worker to subtly offer 'pro-active' advice regarding the risks of dealing in certain items. As this example indicates an educator should not passively await an opportunity to broach a topic or issue.

Although advice may be sought in group settings, it is generally given and requested within one-to-one encounters. And, it is in the context of such encounters where the advice process may overlap and even blur with both guidance and counselling frameworks, which we shall look at more closely. First, however, it is important to briefly look at mentoring within this setting.

What is mentoring?

As noted previously mentoring has acquired a significant presence within work with young people in recent years (Colley 2003; Philip 2008). In particular many organisations have secured funding to establish discrete mentoring programmes. This trend prompts three questions. First, what is mentoring? Second, why has it 'taken-off' and acquired such a high profile in the space of little more than a decade? Third, how does it relate to wider youth work practice?

The popular idea of 'mentor' stems from the eponymous character in Ancient Greek literature who was chosen and entrusted by a father to guide, advise and educate his son while he was away. It is to this spirit of guidance and advising that modern-day mentors are supposed to look to. Formal mentoring has several possibilities; there may be learning mentors, academic mentors, peer mentors and professional mentors. Here in the United Kingdom, the National Mentoring Network (NMN) offers up several interesting definitions of a formal mentor as being:

1. A person who wants to help another person develop and grow – someone who will get to know them, give them advice and encouragement and share with them their own school or work experience (NMN 2000).
2. A one-to-one, non-judgemental relationship in which an individual voluntarily gives time to support and encourage another. This is typically developed at a time of transition in the mentee's life and lasts for a significant and sustained period of time (Shiner *et al.* 2004).
3. A process by which an older and more experienced person takes a younger person under his/her wing, freely offering advice, support and encouragement. The older person (mentor) becomes, among other things, a role model who inspires the younger person (mentee) (*ibid.*).

These definitions share a number of characteristics. First, they view mentoring in a positive way, as a means of reaching out and helping young people. Second, they see it as inherently an individualised relationship, unlike youth work which historically has been built upon and around collective encounters. Third, many mentoring programmes are 'crisis led'. The young person being offered a mentor at a point in time when they have either 'been in trouble' or experienced a crisis of some sort. This is not universally the case for programmes can cast a far wider net but this is rare. Funding often requires mentoring programmes to focus attention on young people who are judged to be 'disadvantaged', 'at risk' or 'vulnerable', or who are experiencing troubled or troublesome 'transitions'.

Why mentoring?

Mentoring programmes for young people are increasingly becoming more formally structured. However, this must not encourage us to overlook the many instances where less formal mentoring takes place. Much of this is valued by young people and is helpful. However, it is argued that within certain communities the over-riding social ethos means many adults who might informally 'mentor' young people may encourage them to engage in 'risky', even criminal activities (Osgood *et al.* 2005). Therefore, formal programmes are seen as especially helpful in areas where, for example, there is below-average take-up of post-compulsory education, low expectations in relation to employment or high rates of criminality. Mentoring tends to work from a foundation of mutuality, trust, support and even friendship. Critics of formal mentoring programmes though argue that mentoring is too often about tracking, surveillance and social control of young people (Philip 2000). In the United States pioneering mentoring programmes have long been working with young people from the former foundation (Rhodes 2002). Here mentors tend to be viewed and valued as 'non-parent adults' that encourage supportive meaningful relationships with young people that impact in a positive way. Equally, mentees are viewed as being young people possessing unfulfilled potential with a positive contribution to make both in society and in their own personal lives (Freedman 1993).

Briefly, work carried out by Rhodes in the United States looks extensively into the interventionist approach of youth mentoring programmes and concludes that good mentoring relationships can contribute to positive youth development (Rhodes 1994). She argues the case for youth mentoring programmes in view of shifting economic, social and cultural conditions that have eroded opportunities for inter-generational contact in modern-day America. Here, Rhodes is referring to the point that too many adolescents fail to form positive connections with caring adults mainly because of rising one-parent households, cuts in school budgets that reduce child/adult ratios and declining neighbourhood safety that can feed the social isolation of children and young people (Rhodes 2002). Rhodes insists that these programmes can make a contribution towards overcoming the loss of natural mentors in the community (see also Putnam 2000; Scales *et al.* 2001). It is to this aspect of fostering young people's health and well-being that good youth mentoring programmes subscribe to. Mentoring, however, takes a number of forms and for that reason it is important to consider the two that have had most impact within the British setting.

Peer mentoring

Peer mentoring programmes are now becoming commonplace in many schools. Initially developed in the United States, these programmes prepare groups of young people to act as mentors and advisers to other students within the institution. These are designed to help tackle issues such as bullying, racism, low self-esteem, friendship problems and inadequate sexual health awareness as well as offering a means of providing learning support. In one school, with which the author has been involved, the Big Sisters programme is addressing among other issues bullying in the school. According to the programme facilitator, peer mentoring 'gives young women a space to think about their behaviour and actions and helps them to bring about a change hopefully for the better'. A current Big Sister explains how

> being on the programme made me realise just how bad I was getting when deep down I really didn't want to be like that... you know a bully. Now, I try to stick up for other girls when the cussing and fighting starts.

Students undergo training to become peer mentors and many are keen to volunteer their services for a variety of reasons. The programme operates not only in the host school but encourages students to become mentors to other young people attending different schools. For example, as one explained:

> Because I was bullied in the annexe and didn't have no one to turn to I know what it feels like. So, for me being a peer mentor is about helping those other people so that they don't suffer what I did.
>
> (Ronni, aged 17)

Another told the author:

> I really enjoy it because I want to be a PE teacher so I've been able to mentor local primary school kids around football and rugby sessions.
>
> (Donna, aged 17)

A third told:

> It's a good experience to have and will look good on my CV when I'm applying for University or for jobs.
>
> (Laverne, aged 18)

Learning mentors

Unlike peer mentoring, learning mentor programmes have for some time received substantial funding from the government (Cruddas 2005). They have been designed to help tackle above-average levels of academic failure among certain groupings of pupils, notably those living in inner-city areas and working-class and Afro-Caribbean males. *The Excellence in Cities* (EiC) Initiative launched in 1999 by the Department for Education and Employment placed learning mentors in selected inner-city schools to raise attainment, to reduce barriers to learning and to address rising truancy and exclusion rates. It is important to avoid confusion with regard to the use of the term as it is employed to describe paid staff employed to undertake learning support work within schools (Cruddas 2005) as well as volunteers meeting with a student for an hour or so once a week or fortnight. However, both will usually work to set curricular programmes that are time-limited and outcome-orientated. They are also expected to work only with young people identified by staff as being 'at risk' or in danger of becoming socially excluded. But there are also learning mentor programmes that focus on the so-called gifted and talented or highest performing students.

As the proportion of young people involved in full-time education has risen so has the involvement of youth workers in educational institutions and programmes. In particular, school- and college-based youth workers are frequently responsible for co-ordinating mentoring programmes as well as for providing one-to-one support for students. Centre-based workers are also managing homework clubs that employ learning mentors. Youth work has found itself via these and other developments responsible not merely for managing traditional mentoring projects but also peer and learning mentor programmes. Much of this engagement has been funding-driven but with the integration of youth workers into multi-professional teams and the growth of personalised learning it is inevitable that for the foreseeable future mentoring will remain an activity closely allied to youth work.

In conclusion

Within this chapter I have explored the variations between mentoring and advice and how generic advice and mentoring operate within a professional youth work setting. Now I will consider some of the commonalities between the two.

Professional youth workers and informal educators fulfil a variety of roles and from time to time don various hats. For example, a youth worker may take on the role of advocate, counsellor, guide or mentor when working alongside young people. In fact, they frequently opt to combine all four within their everyday practice. Indeed, when does a youth worker stop being a counsellor and become a guide? When does a youth worker stop advocating in order to begin mentoring? Certainly given that youth workers teach as much by example as by the word, it can be said, with a degree of truth, that they continually place mentoring at the heart of their practice.

Although there appears to be clear differences between the disciplines, everyday practice examples from the field illustrate the common threads between them. Below are three extracts taken from interviews with practitioners:

> To me, youth work is too simplistic a label given the areas of work we have to cover. I mean most of us are covering areas such as counselling, restorative justice, work with young offenders, personal advising . . . The list seems to go on and on!
>
> (local authority youth worker)

> You just can't say that we do one thing or the other. We are now expected to be multi-skilled in lots of ways – counselling, mentoring, community, transition etc. Plain old youth work don't exist anymore if ever it did.
>
> (project worker for voluntary organisation)

> A lot of what we do with young people encompasses a variety of skills namely advocacy, counselling and mentoring. In my role for Connexions I seem to do all of these along with more social work-type things.
>
> (Connexions Personal Advisor)

What emerges from all the above is the need for workers to have not merely a clear grasp of the different roles but also a thorough working knowledge of how they mesh within everyday practice. Not least because practice so often demands the capacity to move seamlessly between roles, offering advice and information, counselling and mentoring all within the context of one encounter.

9 | Enhancing group life and association

Gill Patton

This chapter examines the potential benefits of group life and association within youth work. In doing so Gill Patton looks briefly at the history of group work with its emphasis on voluntary associations and communities organising themselves for their own benefit. The encouragement of groups and associational life can be seen as a foundation for democratic ways of life and holds the potential for engaging with wider political processes. From there she turns to recent research highlighting individual and civic benefits of belonging to groups and then on to some practice issues.

In this chapter I want to explore how group process can be more beneficial in many circumstances than one-to-one work; and why support for group work should be prioritised as a continuing way of working with all young people, whether viewed as 'included' or 'at risk of exclusion'. This is particularly important at a time when individualism is increasing and distrust is growing within our communities and society in general.

Joining in

It has been noted that young people like to gather in social groups to 'plan and organise their own social activities' (Gordon 1989: 14). They meet informally, for example, in bus shelters, shopping centres and around park benches. This seems to be particularly true for young people approaching or experiencing adolescence (Barton and Barton 2007). They gain much from the informal social interaction – and being with each other is rewarding in itself (Hirsch 2005). Within these informal groups members 'have conscious, significant, decision making power over the affairs of the group' (Gordon 1989: 14). There are emotional and biological rewards of being in groups. A sense of connectedness or community with others can result. As Milson (1982: 15) argued, happiness is rarely found in isolation and the 'building of bridges between our own lives and those in our significant circle' is fundamental. This is perhaps something we know from experience and increasingly this theory is supported by research.

In more recent debates it has been the work of Robert D. Putnam and his associates that has set the scene. Putnam (2000: 19) uses the notion of social capital (meaning connections among individuals and the social networks and the norms of reciprocity and trustworthiness that arise from them). He is able to show that considerable individual and social benefits arise where communities have a significant stock of social capital. He has also shown that there has been a decline in social capital in the United States, and that there are marked variations between different neighbourhoods and areas. Previous research by Putnam in Italy (1993) revealed that there were clear 'civic' and 'uncivic' areas within regions in the country. He portrayed civic communities as having an interest and active participation in 'public issues'. This he described as civic engagement. He also argued they had greater political equality marked by 'horizontal relations of reciprocity and cooperation' as opposed to 'vertical relations of authority and dependency' (1993: 88). He found that these 'civic' areas also benefited from solidarity, trust and tolerance relying on recognition that people were dependent on each other. Overall, there was a focus on collective rather than individual gain, with pathways to wider political systems.

Of further significance to youth work is Putnam's argument that being part of groups impacts significantly on individual health and well-being. Increasing evidence from neuroscience supports the idea that our emotional health impacts upon all areas of our lives, including our physical health. If we are optimistic and confident we increase our chances of good health, and friendship networks and feeling close to other people are major contributors to our feelings of well-being. Goleman (1993) argues that poor emotional health is linked to such illnesses as heart disease and cancer. Using a significantly stronger statistical basis, Putnam was able to show considerable benefits from group membership. The finding that has gained the most attention concerned smoking. 'As a rough rule of thumb', Putnam (2000: 331) concluded, 'if you belong to no groups but decide to join one, you cut your risk of dying over the next year *in half*. If you smoke and belong to no groups, it's a toss-up statistically whether you should stop smoking or start joining' (emphasis in the original). It has also been noted by Elsdon *et al.* (1995) in their large-scale research into involvement in voluntary organisations that one of the greatest benefits is personal growth and an increasing sense of confidence. As Goleman (1993), again, argues, difficulties in relationships are a trigger for depression particularly in young people. One of the most worrying aspects of Putnam's research concerns the decline of social capital in the United States. He found, for example, declining political and civic engagement, a significant decrease in informal social ties and a lowering of tolerance and trust over the last 25 years of the twentieth century. It seems unlikely that there has been such a sharp decline in Britain – but there is increasing evidence of a greater turnover in membership of organisations, and of a growing class polarisation, with professional and managerial groups being significantly more likely to join formal groups (Warde *et al.* 2004). There is also increasing evidence concerning a deepening individualistic orientation in society. It may be that this has arisen in part from a significant increase in individualised leisure activities (especially watching TV). Arguably, this pattern within society will continue with the power of mass media and mass forms of communication. Of particular note, however, has been the growing emphasis on consumption and lifestyle – and the ways these have been conditioned by globalisation. Increasing globalisation has produced the 'eradication of autonomous cultures, but simultaneously the elimination of the boundaries within which communities are or were constructed' (Jeffs and Smith 2002). One unfortunate consequence of this has been a growing risk of depression for young people and a more general feeling of unhappiness in richer countries (Lane 2000; Layard 2005; UNICEF 2007). Being part of a group organised around interests or locality can build confidence, self-esteem and develop our relationships.

Group work

Workers with young people were among the first to develop 'group work' as a specialism and separate area of activity. The development of work with youth people – in the form of clubs, uniformed organisations and fellowships – is taken by many commentators as laying the foundations for the emergence of a self-conscious group work (see, for example, Reid 1981). Many of those who began to fashion group work theory in the United States had experience of working with youth groups (e.g., Eduard C. Lindeman and Grace Coyle). Eduard C. Lindeman, for example, saw group work as a 'mental hygiene experience – a venture in sanity' (cited in Konopka 1972: vii). He recognised that belonging to, and playing our part in, groups was fundamental to the quality of people's lives and integral to their well-being.

In Britain it was those working in youth work who first recognised and championed group work theory (e.g., Josephine Macalister Brew and Peter Kuenstler), and much of the popularisation of social group work in the 1960s and early 1970s is down to the contribution of youth work trainers such as Fred Milson (1963), Joan Matthews (1966), Leslie Button (1974) and Bernard Davies (1975). Given the contribution of youth work to the development of group work it is all the sadder that in recent years we have witnessed a 're-branding youth work as a form of individualised case-management' (Jeffs and Smith 2002: 55) and to a great deal of it being focused on the achievement of personal certificated outcomes. Therefore, the definition and role of many working in youth services has altered accordingly. In most cases this is led by concerns around social control and is outcome-based. Interventions have increasingly been aimed at 'those at risk' and 'those most likely to be excluded', but in reality there is a huge debate as to whether they have the ability to support those that are excluded or are at risk of being excluded.

The increased focus on work with individuals, combined with the requirement to target, and to accredit outcomes, has led to a declining use of the forms of free-flowing group work that long characterised youth work. It has also led to a growing failure on the part of youth services to properly attend to the cultivation of social capital. The lessons from the United States in this respect are clear. A number of programmes aimed at the prevention of specific problems such as drug use or violence have not been successful. In fact, it is argued that some only compounded the difficulties increasing the likelihood of the behaviour (Goleman 1993). In England, one of the main interventions – Connexions – was also arguably more likely to isolate and stigmatise (Jeffs and Smith 2002). Although nationally Connexions has been dismantled, this mode of working, like the brand, survives. Despite its manifest limitations, not least an inability to reach the most excluded young people, and support and develop them as individuals in a holistic way on an ongoing basis. The natural course of events within groups is that a range of issues appear when young people are together and talking (Jeffs and Smith 2005). The potential for accessing a number of issues and the richness of group work can be seen as offering various benefits that certain targeted interventions cannot offer. A lot of other targeted work is also restrictive in that it only works with those young people who are at 'risk of exclusion' on a one-to-one interaction where the young person becomes a client. Often a group of excluded young people are thrown together in some kind of support group. Some of this work has benefits but it is difficult to call it youth work, which has always been identified by voluntary relationships, informal education and an emphasis on process (Jeffs and Smith 2005). Research by the Youth

Justice Board found that 'youth culture' has a greater impact on young people than their personality or history. In areas where there is a disparity in income between people and these inequalities 'co-exist without a sense of community' there is greater risk of becoming involved in street crime. Interventions such as 'Splash-Plus' have had some success in 'the shifting of priorities' with young people but these have been short term and led by aims of diversionary activities (Youth Justice Board 2003: see also Harris 1998).

Association

For a significant period of time 'association' was overtly one of the defining features of youth work. The Albemarle Report (Ministry of Education 1960) advocated, for example, that the main aims of the youth service should be 'association, training and challenge'. It argued that young people's social needs should be met 'before their needs for training and formal instruction' (1960: 52). It also argued that the youth service:

> should seek first to provide places for association in which young people may maintain and develop, in the face of a disparate society, their sense of fellowship, of mutual respect and tolerance. Such centres may also help to counteract the increasing educational and professional stratification of society. Those who are intellectually or financially well-endowed have as much to gain as others from the opportunity for mixed fellowship, as much to learn from as to give to others. It is very difficult to run a club whose members have mixed educational backgrounds, but it is exceptionally well worth trying.
>
> (1960: 36–37)

Such sentiments fell out of favour as youth services and organisations struggled to make sense of the changing experiences of young people in the 1980s and the 1990s (and especially their changing social habits) and to make a case for youth work to the government and other funders who had become predominantly concerned with targeted, outcome-driven work (Robertson 2005).

There is a need to reclaim and promote a focus on the educative power of social movements and voluntary associations. Historically, associations have developed because of our ever-evolving society created agencies that wanted to support people, but with an emphasis on self-help and 'citizen action' (Konopka 1972). We need to learn again from those youth groups and agencies who have a strong sense of participation and 'fellowship'. Some of these organisations were supported by state resources (although often only in a limited way), but most had a clear emphasis on improving the 'lot' of others by involvement not by acting on behalf of others, or doing 'to' others. Organisations such as churches, tenants groups and YMCAs have always had associational structures where people are included in decision-making at some level. Moreover, many of them were created to represent people's interests and in that sense have the potential to link into larger political processes. Settlement houses, neighbourhood centres, scouts and YMCAs, for example, were led by a commitment to democratic ways and processes (Konopka 1972) and the fostering of fellowship and community (Jeffs and Smith 2002). These ideas are clearly outlined in the statement agreed at the 21st National Convention of the YMCA held in 1958: 'Members take part in developing the life of the Association through the democratic process of shared responsibility and cooperative effort. Through group experience, opportunities are provided for individuals to grow and become responsible leaders and citizens' (cited in Konopka 1972: 181).

As Knowles (1950) puts it, groups can become spaces where the experience of living co-operatively can exist. This creates, what Alexis de Tocqueville (1848) refers to as, 'habits of the heart' which enable people to be connected to others and the wider community. He refers to these associational gatherings as 'laboratories of democracy'. The experience of associations 'helps to sustain friendships' (Smith 1994: 152). Those people with connections to others are more likely to be tolerant, empathetic and less cynical. Without the opportunities to test out their views, what they like and who they are people will see the worst in life and in others. As Lindeman notes, when 'people have thought and felt and lived democracy there has been cast upon human experience a sharp luminosity. Fears were dispelled and hopes renewed . . . whenever . . . . tyranny and despotism have succeeded to power, human experience has been shadowed by suspicion, anger and bitterness' (cited in Konopka 1972). As well as being good for our mental health he sees the small group as a 'leadership laboratory' and a place for 'nuclear democracy'.

Goleman argues that living and practicing emotional and social intelligence, with its emphasis on empathy, understanding, tolerance and acceptance, allows people to live together with mutual respect. This creates 'the possibility of productive public discourse' and is the 'art of democracy'. He argues that school is central in providing this but there is also a clear role for the youth work. Many young people become excluded from school or the system does not meet their needs in terms of how they learn. Gordon (1989) describes a group of unemployed young men who were seen to have 'failed' by the standards of the formal education system yet had succeeded in securing funding for a music project. The youth service, and the place it offers in nurturing groups on a voluntary basis, was important here – young people can really have the opportunity to live with the commitment to moral and civic values. This level of investment is beneficial in the long term as associational life can make a significant difference to communities. As Smith (2001b) points out, communities will benefit from lower crime figures, better health, higher educational achievement and better economic growth when linked by the idea of social capital.

Fostering group life and association

Getting groups together relies to a significant extent upon workers getting to know 'key people' in the community and using 'the grapevine' of networks that already exist, as 'word of mouth' is the most effective way to 'recruit' people (Smith 1994: 116). A sense of safety and familiarity is important here. Being around and being seen is essential (*ibid.*: 9). It is even more important for those that are isolated or for communities of interest rather than locality. Making young people feel welcome, important and valued is essential. Sharing ideas and views can make people feel included; it fosters the view that others like me exist and share my thoughts and feelings, in turn fostering a feeling of acceptance and understanding. This can have a powerful impact and as noted in earlier chapters it is particularly important during adolescence to gain this sense of belonging.

The very beauty of group life is that it is hard to predict what learning and benefits will come from being part of a group. Youth work remains central to providing opportunities for group experiences. As Jeffs and Smith put it, the 'central concern should be to work with others so that they may organise and take responsibility' (2005: 25–26). No doubt some outcomes could be set out but there is a whole layer of learning that cannot be described, or for that matter prescribed, as each group interaction is unique. This relies on youth workers placing trust in conversation and having the confidence to 'go with the flow'. They also need to be careful to be open to the ideas that young people present through this process (Gordon 1989: 17). It is also important to remember that such group work does not have to happen in designated spaces but can happen anywhere (Crimmens *et al.* 2004).

Young people who are negatively labelled in other environments can be equal and active members of a youth group. There is no stigmatisation and they are not 'the client' in the associational experience. For this, and other reasons, a focus on power relations in groups is important. The group itself is vital to the process and has a central role and a responsibility with regard to inclusion and exclusion. We can easily fall into the trap of focusing on an individual to the detriment of others' experiences within the group. We need to involve groups in thinking about and taking on responsibility for what they do and say. Peer group pressure can work in a positive, supportive way and the opportunities for inclusion can increase and self-esteem built through the process of group work and association. At the same time we need to attend to the negative aspects of group and associational life – especially where members look to bonding with each other rather than building bridges to others outside the group (see Robertson 2005).

It is often the most challenging for young people who are first removed from the youth club or avoided on the street by detached youth workers. This is understandable as groups and clubs are not always easy if a disruptive element is continually impacting on the members and other young people. However, as we know, they are often the young people who most need membership of a group – and who can if encouraged make a significant contribution. Reid argues that the group can work as a 'vehicle for ameliorating maladaptive behaviour' (1981: xvi). By excluding young people, or hoping that a support worker will on a one-to-one or targeted group basis pick them up, we eradicate the opportunity to involve them. Exclusion increases and the experience of being around a mixture of young people and thereby developing social skills and confidence through interaction with their peers will be lost. The children and young people who have always felt excluded, isolated and withdrawn, unable to develop the social skills to survive in groups, will miss out again on the positive feelings that other young people will experience by the simple process of being with others and sharing a common experience in a group.

There was an example of a young man who would persistently interrupt activities or conversations with comments. Sometimes the young people would laugh, other times they would tell him to shut up. If he was laughed at the young man continued until he became too disruptive. Once told to shut up the young man would retaliate at which point other young people would join in to protect the young person who had tried to stop the disruptive behaviour and enable the group to function. The conflict would escalate and the young man who interrupted, probably to be more included, was left feeling even more excluded. As a worker it was a difficult situation to manage, trying not to exclude any member in this process, but often it ended up with attempting to talk to the disruptive young person individually, getting to know them, their interests and their background, trying to connect to build some trust. As in this case workers may need to re-think how they operate in groups. Often one-to-one work takes over to the detriment of the group experience. Moreover, it is necessary to ask whether they perpetuate exclusion by seeking to help particularly disruptive young people with various strategies that focus on certain aspects of their personality. The power of the collective group, the simple process of sharing views and opinions, being given the power to make decisions as a group and shape their experience is, we should always remember, a highly creative and dynamic process. One that wherever possible should be allowed the opportunity to develop and flourish.

Trusting in the group and its richness is important and the strength lies in the variety of different personalities, strengths and weaknesses of individual young people. Modelling and developing empathy within the group is a useful strategy. Encouraging this from children and young people helps them understand each other and remain supportive through the most disruptive times. This helps build acceptance and tolerance; differences can be understood within the context of similarities, and young people come to understand that others are like me but also different from me.

Diversity within groups is also one of the most powerful strategies in celebrating difference. For example, a withdrawn young person can learn that their views and opinions are valid through the group process. It makes sense then to have certain skills role modelled by others and give the opportunity for those skills to be developed. Workers must be careful to ensure inclusion as much as possible as the group can provide a space to develop those. As Reid (1981: xvi) points out, the group experience can enhance the individuals social skills and values of the larger society.

In conclusion

As we have seen much youth work has always been based on voluntary participation and informal education with a clear emphasis on democracy and association. At a very basic level some policy initiatives have recognised the importance of friendships in terms of our sense of health and well-being. Youth workers are potentially well placed to support and encourage young people in groups. However, the group provides the opportunity for much more than this – the development of valuable social skills and attitudes such as listening, understanding and empathy. Attributes that cannot be learnt from a computer programme or acquired in isolation from others. Youth workers can maximise the potential of young people who meet in groups and set down the foundation for practicing democracy. In turn this can create the pathways to wider political processes. An increasingly complex society needs a response from youth work – one that places group life at the core of youth provision. In fact, it is essential at this time when the 'fabric of society seems to unravel at ever greater speed, when selfishness, violence, and a meanness of spirit seem to be rotting the goodness of our communal lives' (Goleman 1993: xii). Recognising the importance of 'youth culture' in shaping young people's choices and experiences gives the opportunity for youth work organisations to promote an alternative way of living within communities – a culture that places emphasis on association and democratic ways of life that the group can provide.

10 | Working with faith

Howard Nurden

A high proportion of youth work has always been sponsored and supported by faith organisations. Currently in Britain a majority of youth workers are employed by such organisations. However, it is not only those employed by faith-based agencies who are called upon to discuss and debate matters of a spiritual nature with young people. Questions such as 'Where is God?' and 'Who made God?' cannot be easily answered. Responses to them, whatever form they take, require faith. Effective work with young people will encourage an exploration of questions that can only be responded to with further questions. At times such as these youth work enters into the realm of faith.

Plato thought the physical sun was the best symbol for his God. Today there are many expressions of faith. In the United Kingdom 5 per cent of the population identify themselves as belonging to non-Judeo-Christian faiths (Johal 2003: 1). The majority of these are aged below 30. It is essential to recognise that working with faith in a youth work context is not only about Christian youth work. However, I will declare this chapter predominately draws from the Christian approaches to youth work in its exploration of working with faith. This is largely because this is the tradition I most intimately know. Nevertheless it will hopefully relate to other contexts.

Towards an understanding

Terms such as spirituality, spiritual growth, faith, faith development and religion are not easily defined. Yet it is important to work towards an understanding of them in order to get a sense of the issues being discussed here. Draper and Draper (2000: 19) claim we are experiencing the largest culture shift in the 'West' for over two centuries and that this has a profound effect on the manifestation of faith. The cultural environment in which the teenage years are lived out has changed. Attitudes towards family, institutions, education and media are different (Margo *et al.* 2006). Levels of choice have multiplied and a greater value is being placed in having the freedom to choose. This shift has led to new attitudes towards belief and truth.

> It used to be said, 'It is true, therefore it works'. It was then said, 'It works, therefore it is true'. Now it's, 'It works, and that is all there is to it!'
>
> (Hickford 1998: 84)

Belief has become more of a commodity, in a culture where all meaning is relative and unifying 'truths' are viewed with suspicion. The change in social forces from modernity to post-modernity is a move from a culture where identity is found through production to a culture based on consumption (Cray 1998: 4). Consumerism is central to young people's experience of the world. Cray (1998: 5) describes shopping malls as the new community centres, recognising spirituality within consumerism as it offers to meet inner needs through pleasure. An identity revolving around leisure, image and consumption is not stable. A result of this is an upsurge of interest in spirituality (Cray 1998: 13; Thatcher 1999: 1; Francis and Roberts 2005). McAllister believes this is because some young people 'are disenchanted with the emptiness around them' (1999: 154). Faith-based youth work struggles to exist within this culture when it operates from institutions that are mistrusted or seen as irrelevant. But work with young people that offers purpose, an alternative identity construct and an environment to explore meaning can provide an antidote to some of the negative effects a post-modern culture has on young people.

Hay and Nye (1998: 5) define spirituality as an awareness of God, while other writers view it as being an aesthetic experience or a heightened awareness of oneself and others. Similarly Eastman (2002: 2) describes spirituality as the inter-relatedness of emotional, cognitive and intuitive self. Both of the texts just quoted agree that all have a potential for spirituality. Spirituality cannot be scientifically 'proved' but may be a vital part of our make-up. It requires belief in something outside of our physical being, an awareness of ourselves, others, the world and God. It is often expressed through 'mountain-top' experiences and brings with it the idea of pilgrimage and journey. If spirituality is something we all have, then it needs to be nourished, developed and grown. Strommer *et al.* (2001: 156) state that spiritual development is about Biblical teaching, a commitment to Jesus, seeing God at work in changed lives. However, in *Youth A Part*, a study commissioned by the Church of England to explore the relationship between young people and the church, a distinction is made between religious and spiritual development. The latter being defined as:

Getting in touch with the deeper parts of life – valuing the experiences of awe and wonder, of hurt and sorrow, relationships with other people and the natural world, and coming to an understanding of what is meant by the term 'God'.

(Cattermole, quoted Church of England 1996: 40)

This recognises that all young people are searching for spirituality or meaning. Spiritual development should be about growth in an individual's capacity, experience, understanding and response. Lee defines spiritual development as being 'about each person as a unique human being with life-long potential for growth and development – an ability to learn, through reflection on experience, about self, others and the creation of which we are all a part' (1999: 1). Such a definition reads a bit like the mission statement of a youth organisation, which would need to be interpreted into action to achieve youth work aims.

Faith is different to spirituality. Dallow suggests a definition of faith might be 'the commitment or belief and resulting actions that we put around our spirituality like a framework' (2002: 80). Faith involves belief and a sense of trust, but also leads to action. It is necessary to make sense of one's faith by fitting it into a pattern of values, beliefs and ideas (Kinast 1999: 3–7). This need not be about slavish conformity but about developing a way of living consistent to one's faith view. He goes on to explore the need to secure a balance between meaning (the subjective) and facts (the objective), and identifies how difficult this is to achieve. Langford (1982) sums this dilemma up well in identifying the continuum between blind faith and rationality, with the balance being unblind faith. There must be grounds for faith, but not proof; there must be room for belief. Jesus, for example, did not teach in absolute truths, but used story and answered questions with questions. Like that of Socrates', Jesus' approach was to encourage individuals to discover truth for themselves. Faith is the living out of belief; it should be evident in the lives of believers. Truth is not easy to find; searching involves faith. Doubt is part of this search; the opposite of faith is faithlessness not doubt. This implies our faith, like our spirituality, can develop.

Theories of faith development have been put forward, such as Westerhoff (1980), looking at the process of faith not the content. Westerhoff identifies experienced faith, affiliative faith, searching faith and owned faith, claiming that faith is real no matter what stage it may be at. These theories identify patterns and recognise faith as a journey.

In Hinduism our existence is seen, both in this life and beyond, as a journey. Some, for example Christians who believe that a conversion experience is central to the Christian faith, while agreeing with the concept of faith development, would argue that faith must be found before it can be developed.

Faith is personal and throughout history various religions have grown up around different expressions of faith. This leads to challenging questions such as – 'Is every expression and exploration of spirituality equally valid?' I'm not sure that an answer is required in order to work towards spiritual growth and faith development, which is about the growth and development of individuals, communities and wider society. But religions do make judgements about whether people are 'in' or 'out':

> Religion is about identity and identity excludes. For every 'We' there is a 'Them', the people not like us. There are kin and non-kin, friends and strangers, brothers and others, and without these boundaries it is questionable whether we have an identity at all.

> (Sacks 2002: 46)

Experiences of faith can lead to the setting up of modes of behaviour such as in the Jewish *Torah* or the Islamic *shari'ah*, which set out both ritual and moral codes (W. C. Smith 1962: 179). Religious faith throughout history and in a variety of contexts has been a vehicle for exclusion and discrimination, at times with awful consequences. Moral judgements cannot be set aside and ultimately faith will be judged by the faithless not by its' truth, which by definition cannot be proved, but by the actions it inspires. An example of this is Gandhi; his message was morally compelling and one that he lived out (see Stuart 2006).

Historical perspective

From the early nineteenth century onwards, philanthropic individuals, many of whom were Christian, created and supported youth organisations. Motivated by their Christian faith they viewed this work as a natural expression of their beliefs. However, there was an illiberal and intolerant strand running through much early Christian youth work. Many Christian organisations actively sought to eradicate provision offered by those with differing views, for example, the intemperate attacks on Hannah More for being a clandestine Methodist or Robert Owen for being a non-believer who, it was said, allowed even Roman Catholics to access the buildings he controlled. Often a virulent anti-Semitism was also apparent in these early initiatives. Brierley asks if those providing youth provision were more concerned with the needs of young people or promoting their own beliefs and maintaining their own position (2003: 41). Both were probably true and are reflected in provision today.

> Christians helped pioneer the modern day Youth Service. They engaged with young people at a time when others didn't. Faith was not coincidental to this practice. It influenced their approach.
>
> (Brierley 2003: 41)

Concern about the decline of numbers of young people involved in the Christian, Moslem and Jewish faiths in Britain has led to major soul searching into what can be done to address this. In 2001 The Salvation Army published *The Burden of Youth*, a comprehensive and forward-thinking report into the issues facing young people. However, it could be argued that the motivation for this work came from the desire to ensure the future of the organisation, as much as to address the needs it uncovered.

For the bulk of the last century faith groups remained the dominant youth work provider, although increasingly via a partnership with the state. As the latter's involvement grew so a divide between them emerged. Increasingly the 'statutory sector labelled youth ministry as unprofessional and proselytising' and churches responded with claims 'that statutory youth work was devoid of spiritual significance' (Brierley 2003: 57). It was a process which, Ward suggests, was exacerbated by the development of a youth work profession overwhelmingly committed to the secularisation of practice (1997: 12). *Youth A Part* acknowledges these changes and bemoans the difficulties in establishing effective work with young people when faced with funding uncertainties (Church of England 1996: 151–152). This is especially the case for faith-based initiatives wishing to work esoterically with young people, not fitting the particular targets that are the current flavour.

During the last decade new social policy initiatives have created fresh opportunities for the faith sector to engage with young people (Ahmed *et al.* 2007). For example, youth workers employed to encourage the participation of young Muslims within youth volunteering opportunities or Connexions Personal Advisors being placed in churches. New funding arrangements, especially for targeted interventions, allow the state to set the agenda but these can offer fresh possibilities for partnerships.

Faith-based youth work

Brierley (2003) considers the four values of youth work to have been set out in the *Second Ministerial Conference on the Future of the Youth*

Service held in 1991. These were voluntary participation, informal education, empowerment and equality of opportunity. He makes a strong case that these values can be applied to Christian youth work, justified both theologically and through practice. Brierley adds a fifth value, incarnation, believing this to be the unique contribution of Christian youth work (2003: 135). This concerns the Christian belief that God became fully human in Jesus and so identified with humanity. Both Brierley (2003) and Ward (1997) relate this to work with young people, with the incarnation of Christ inspiring those engaged in youth work to enter the world of young people with sensitivity and respect. Ward argues the purpose of Christian youth work should be to work with those both inside and outside the church (1997: 1). Youth work and youth ministry are often seen as separate entities, with youth ministry being defined in exclusively spiritual terms with a specific aim to preach a message, as opposed to youth work being a broader approach to working with young people. Brierley makes a claim for youth work and ministry to be seen together. He sets out the purpose of this work being to 'promote an opportunity for young people to explore questions of faith and belief for themselves' (2003: 11). For him youth work is ineffective if it does not bring about change, with all youth workers being in the business of conversion. So while the term youth work, as opposed to youth ministry, may be used to describe an alternative primary task, in fact the distinction is less than clear. If faith-based youth work is seeking to be genuinely holistic in its approach to achieving the development of young people, I'm not sure that a distinction exists at all.

How this purpose is translated into the aims for Christian work with young people is debatable. Ashton states, 'the first aim of Christian youth work must be to present a young person with the claims of Jesus Christ' (1986: 68). For him it is not Christian if it does not do this. Aiken (1994) agrees that the aim is to develop followers of Christ, being measured by the changes apparent in the lives of young people. Such an approach sets faith-based work apart from the model outlined by Brierley. However, there are others who take a broader view. Eastman, for example, suggests the aim is 'to encourage people to grow into a stable relationship with God ... to enable them to understand the issues of the world ... to help them understand themselves' (1976: 28). The focus here is on the importance of responding to the needs of young people, encouraging a search for identity and enabling young people to reach maturity.

Theological issues arise from discussion of aims. It is necessary to identify appropriate aims in a dynamic way, seeking to apply Christian understandings to the desire to develop 'whole people'. *Youth A Part*

(Church of England 1996: Chapter 2) is clear about the need for a theology for youth work. Taking Christ as the model, it expands the importance of youth work being about personal development, based on an incarnational approach achieved through relationships with young people.

For Green (1990) theology is a discipline, something a disciple is engaged in. Kinast sees it as being revelation, faith and living (1996: 5). Both describe how theology is developed through reflection. Kinast explains how we make sense of the faith through selecting an experience, attending to our feelings and reflecting (1999: 8–14). Through reflection-on-action, theological understanding develops. All this can be usefully applied to youth work. Theological reflection asks how God is being experienced and expects material to be found within all arenas (Green 1990: 12). This provides an expression of work with young people outside of the narrow aims of preaching a message. A theology for Christian youth work based around the model of working with experience, exploration, reflection and response in order to discover God, therefore, emerges. The aim of this approach is for young people to discover truth and meaning, making sense of the world and God. It encourages questions and takes up a position between the certitude of truth and the uncertainty of experience.

This links to the ideas of spiritual growth and faith development. It provides some challenges to faith-based youth work. Workers will need to consider how they view ultimate truth and whether they wish to present a truth or create a space for truth to be discovered. Ways will need to be found to encourage an exploration of the spiritual, and models made available to provide a framework of faith to go around spiritual understandings. The following sections consider some responses of youth work to these challenges, as it works with the spirituality of this age.

A spiritual age – youth work's response

There has been an upsurge of interest in spirituality in many, perhaps all, late capitalist societies (Thatcher 1990: 1). This is curious considering the fact that secularisation has simultaneously grown. This spirituality has often floated free from religion. As people search for spirituality today it is often not the traditional religions to which they turn. Young people now frequently value experience over propositional truth. Individuals ask whether it works, not whether it is true (Draper and Draper 2000: 18). This culture change means approaches to faith-based work with young people must change as it is necessary to find ways of working that are authentic within contemporary culture. As Green and Green explain, this requires new approaches:

> An alternative way of responding is to reflect on the culture in relation to the rest of society and, being confident of those things that make up the gospel, we become vulnerable but open to the possibility of change.
>
> (2000: 10)

Faith-based youth work should seek to prepare young people for adulthood within the context of today's culture. To do this those working with young people must become fellow pilgrims (Green and Green 2000: 19). In this way the actions of youth workers reflect the theology.

The need for youth work to work in ways that enable young people to explore their spirituality is essential. Work needs to be reflected upon theologically, taking a holistic perspective, being both incarnational and authentic. The concept of journeying together or accompanying (Green and Christian 1998) is a helpful one. Lee identifies four possible spiritual journeys: inwards (self), outwards (others), downwards (environment) and upwards (God) (1999: 16–25). A description of Muslim youth work by Sakina Gul Hussain (undated) illustrates this model. Young Muslims are encouraged to develop their religious identity (self), appreciate the actions of their parents (others), consider the implications of living in a non-Muslim setting (environment) and understand what the Qur'an means (God) (see also Hamid 2006).

An expanding business – the employment of faith-based workers

One of the results of this need to change approach is the expansion in the number of workers employed by faith-based organisations. By 1998, the English Church Attendance Survey found that some 21 per cent of churches had a full-time salaried youth worker (Brierley 2000). This figure may have included some priests and curates who had youth work as their prime responsibility – but it is nonetheless very significant. The most recent figures suggest there are around 5500 full-time equivalent youth workers employed by churches and Christian agencies, more than the statutory youth service (Centre for Youth Ministry 2006). There are also said to be around 100,000 volunteers. Churches have become the largest employer of youth workers in the country (Breirley 2003). This has not happened only through a desire to develop young people's spirituality. Brierley's research also estimates that the church has been losing 1000 under 15s per week, with the number of young people in church halving between 1980 and 2000. Ward (1997: 21–23) sees this rise in employed workers being related to a desire to keep young people and a recognition of the inability to connect with other young people. Whatever the reasons for this expansion it has put Christian youth work back at the heart of youth work. There has also been an important growth of interest in, and practice around, Muslim youth work. For some years there has been work going on – for example, around mosques and various youth associations – sometimes associated with different political groupings (e.g., the Bangladeshi Youth Association). However, in recent years, with much larger numbers of Muslims becoming youth workers, and with an acceptance that significant areas of provision didn't address the needs of different groupings of young Muslims, there has been both a developing literature and some important innovations in practice (Fulat and Jaffrey 2006; Khan 2006).

All this has brought to the fore issues relating to training, funding, management, support and links to other agencies (Ahmed *et al.* 2007: 90). Faith-based youth workers are seeking to develop relationships with young people, sharing their story and making links to God's story. They are attempting to communicate to young people through who they are. How they view the spiritual development of young people varies and is affected by their spiritual perspective and the theology of their employer (Cressey 2007). Tensions in this area include employers seeking to focus the attention of workers upon prioritising the needs of the church and Mosque over those of the young people.

Some examples from practice

What happens in the name of faith-based youth work? The answer to this is a varied one as all sorts of different methods are encountered. However, to convey something of the breadth and variety of approaches I will explore briefly three examples of current work – one programme-based, another focusing on the development of relationships and finally one seeking to offer new experiences. These are not mutually exclusive, although in my experience work with young people tends to be based on one or other of these approaches.

Ward (1997) identifies 'inside-out' youth work, starting with a group of young people connected to the life of the local church. A programme will be offered to this group, perhaps in the form of a youth group or fellowship. This may be what children graduate to after Sunday school. Such programmes tend to be a combination of social activities, teaching, prayer and worship. The aim of such programmes is to build up individuals in the faith. Participants are often strongly encouraged to bring their friends along. Schemes such as *Youth Alpha* and *Youth*

Emmaus, which seek to provide an exploration of the Christian faith, may be used (see Hunt 2004). There are lots of resources on offer providing programme ideas and approaches, such as those contained within the monthly *Youthwork* magazine. They seek to socialise young people into church or faith, but often struggle to engage with the majority outside. A typical session might be based on a theme, such as understanding a Christian perspective on illegal drug misuse, and include introductory activities, the use of a video clip or piece of music to generate discussion, looking at relevant Bible passages and encouraging the young people to relate their conclusions to their lives. Such a session would be planned in advance and delivered in the main by those working with the group. Over a period of time a variety of topics would be covered alongside Bible-based themes.

'Relationships are the fuel on which youth work travels' (Ward 1997: 43). *Youth A Part* (Church of England 1996) outlines some places where relationships with young people can be developed including in churches, schools or night clubs or through detached work. The importance of encouraging positive peer relationships is stressed. Faith can be nurtured through relationships for as Hickford explains 'Christianity is better caught than taught' (1998: 114). A youth worker will seek to nurture good relationships that enable them to come alongside individuals, role modelling the faith within the relationship that they develop (see Smith and Smith 2008). Most people when asked to describe what led them to a faith describe a person, or set of relationships, rather than a theory or structure of beliefs.

The third example seeks to offer young people new and perhaps alternative experiences. It is a challenge for those working with young people to make available a range of experiences enabling an exploration of the spiritual. For some workers the goal lies in the creation of sacred spaces and alternative worship experiences, which are culturally appropriate and multi-sensory (Draper and Draper 2000). Lee (1999) extols the virtues of creativity and silence in creating environments that encourage spiritual development. An example of this approach is the Labyrinth prayer walks that have been available at a variety of cathedrals in the United Kingdom. Participants are given time and space to respond for themselves to specially chosen pieces of poetry, video clips or images, and encouraged to reflect on their lives, their relationships, their environment and their God. A different example is the National Youth Agency inter-faith consultation project (2003–2004) that promoted the value of inter-faith activities and dialogue, offering experiences to encourage a fresh outlook on issues which impact the lives of young people (see also Green 2005).

These examples represent something of a continuum from working in ways that teach faith to ways that encourage a spiritual experience. All approaches along this continuum are valid and will be chosen according to the aims and context of the work. Attention should be paid to creating an environment conducive to the culture of the young people and appropriate to the purpose of the work. Young people should be engaged with and should develop relationships with workers who journey alongside them. Experiences should be offered that encourage them to think and feel differently; they should be enabled to learn through reflecting on these experiences.

Working with faith – some closing thoughts

Faith-based youth work should offer opportunities for young people to explore spiritual issues. This should be built upon a sound, thought through theological base informed by reflection on scripture, tradition, practice and community.

Faith-based youth work must be authentic, offering experiences that lead to fresh understandings and be built on relationships. Faith-based work with young people will include the spiritual. God's presence in the lives of workers and young people may remain a mystery but should not be underestimated. The importance of encouraging a search for God makes faith-based work distinctive. However, while it may be tempting to separate 'faith-based' and 'secular', the value of doing so must be questioned. Faith-based youth work occurs in a variety of settings. It seeks change, both in individuals and in relation to social justice. Above all workers seek to journey alongside young people to enable their growth and development.

Working with faith is about spiritual development, encouraging young people to go beyond themselves in considering their relatedness to others, to their environment and to God. This work should offer the scaffolding of language and cultural understanding to enable young people to become aware of their spirituality. Reflecting theologically enables spiritual experiences to be identified and understood. It should be made possible for young people to reflect on their experiences in this way, in a manner that both engages and liberates them.

The missionary Vincent Donovan said this to the Masai when they asked him if his tribe had found God: 'No, we have not, for us too He is the unknown

God. But we are searching for Him. I have come a long distance to invite you to search for Him, maybe, together, we will find Him.'

(Pimlott 2001: 16)

Effective faith-based work will encourage young people to think for themselves and take responsibility for their own spiritual developments. It must aim for transformation, through dialogue, which will build bridges of respect and understanding.

11 | Managing and developing youth work

Gill Millar

If managers are to manage youth work effectively they needed to understand its occupational culture. Key features of that culture include a concern with person-centred approaches, a belief in the need to promote active involvement in decision making and the notion of the worker as an activist and campaigner. Gill Millar discusses ways whereby managers can 'take people with them' in building effective youth work organisations. This means looking beyond 'systems' approaches towards a management model sympathetic to the values and culture of youth work.

Management is widely viewed as a generic discipline, one that can be applied to any field of work. Management literature tends to assume that the 'product' being managed makes little difference to the approaches to be utilised. Some writers on managing public services (see, for example, Ranson and Stewart 1994) have pointed out that absence of the profit motive within the public arena impacts on the forms management can take. Subsequently much attention has been focused on the importance of good management in ensuring public services are of a better quality, more responsive to their customers and more cost effective. In the 1990s this movement became known as the *New Managerialism* (Clarke and Newman 1997).

This belief that improved management was the route to the better delivery of services has now dominated public policy and practice for over a decade. Yet in youth work, and probably elsewhere in the public sector, when I did my initial research (Miller 1995) interviewees were reluctant to define what they did as management. That was because they saw 'management' as a concept alien to the youth work arena, despite its inclusion in some of the early key texts on youth work such as Russell and Russell (1932) and Henriques (1933). Now it is recognised as an important and valued element of the work, a point demonstrated in *Transforming Youth Work* (2001), where management is singled out as a key area for investment. As a result, the Department for Education and Skills (DfES) commissioned the Transforming Youth Work Management programmes, delivered to managers in local authority youth services and voluntary organisations in all parts of England. These 8-day programmes covered a wide range of topics including understanding organisations and the external environment, strategic thinking and planning, managing performance, innovation and partnerships (Ford *et al.* 2002).

After years of neglect some aspects of youth work appears to have come to the attention of public policy makers. They see it as a means of re-engaging young people with learning and work, promoting their inclusion within communities and enabling their voices to be heard in decisions affecting their lives. Policy documents, green papers and increased Treasury funding confirm that the government now views youth work as part of the solution to young people's social exclusion (see, for example, HM Treasury 2007). Accordingly services for young people and voluntary organisations have found themselves involved in much more partnership work with other public agencies, in the fields of education, employment, health, social service, community regeneration and crime prevention. Such partnerships tie youth work agencies, statutory and voluntary, to contracts and service level agreements that have become the norm for inter-agency work.

Youth work has always been creative in seeking funding to support its work. Increasingly youth work organisations access external sources of funding. Some local authority youth services reported almost 50 per cent of their total spend comes from external sources (NYA Audit of Local Youth Services 2003). All such sources require accountability for the effective use of the money, and youth work organisations have become accustomed to identifying outcomes, meeting targets and managing budgets efficiently. All this has helped to break down a historic resistance to management. Management has been accepted into the occupational culture of state-sponsored youth work. But what differences have taken place as a consequence of this change? Is there still a need to generate models of management specific to youth work settings?

In preparing this chapter I interviewed senior youth work managers and management consultants involved with youth work organisations. Those conversations and an analysis of the literature have highlighted three key attributes relating to the successful management of youth work:

- Providing an appropriate organisational framework to support the work;
- Vision, leadership and direction;
- Identifying and executing key tasks.

All need to be underpinned by a recognition and acceptance that the environment in which youth work takes place is constantly altering as a consequence of national and local policy shifts, demographic trends, new technology and economic and cultural changes. No organisation or profession can stand still in this climate. Thus managers must build in sufficient flexibility to respond to new opportunities while retaining the core function of youth work as an informal education approach to enabling young people to play an active part in decisions that affect their lives. Each of these will be discussed in this chapter. The topics within each section have been drawn from conversations with youth work managers and analysis of Ofsted reports and other government documents.

Organisational frameworks

Youth work is currently located in a range of organisational settings. These include services based in local education authorities and children's trusts, or other departments of county and unitary authorities , voluntary youth organisations, Connexions, local community-based organisations with a wider community development brief, schools and further education colleges, as well as private companies contracted to run youth services in specific areas. Good and bad practice exists in all these and it is too simplistic to identify one as the ideal 'home' for youth work. However, it may be possible to identify some organisational characteristics that will help to support youth work, as opposed to those that hinder its development and progression.

Positive attitudes to young people

Not all organisations that house youth work projects can claim this: some community organisations, for example, see young people as a problem to be solved, rather than as the next generation of their own community. Some, such as council departments and 'big' charities, will see young people as marginal to their core 'business', only coming into contact with them when they appear as 'problems' to be dealt with. While schools and colleges can provide bases for positive youth work, the ethos of some institutions is built on 'controlling' large numbers in order to deliver a curriculum over which the young people have little say and to achieve externally imposed targets. This often results in conflicts between youth work projects and the institutions within which they are located.

In one community school where the youth work team, though based in a separate community centre, was managed as part of the school establishment, it had been agreed that young people and adults who had achieved awards and qualifications through their involvement in youth work would receive their awards as part of the School Prize Day Celebration. However, when the head teacher discovered that some of those who would receive awards had previously been excluded from school, they were refused permission to come onto the school site to receive their awards. As a result, the youth work team had to hold its own, low-key celebration in the community centre.

Where an organisation encourages positive approaches to listening and responding to young people, youth work is more likely to flourish. Youth work can play a major role in enabling an organisation to develop a more positive approach to young people, by demonstrating that they can make effective contributions within communities. However, organisations that do not develop a positive approach are unlikely to provide a long-term secure home for youth work.

A locally based community organisation on an urban estate successfully bid for Neighbourhood Renewal Fund to develop provision for young people. The main motivation for applying for the money was to solve the 'youth problem' on the estate: fear of crime, 'anti-social behaviour' use of drugs etc. Over a 2-year period youth workers worked with young people both to provide activities and to engage them in the life of the estate, through environmental work, organising community festivals and joint fund-raising with adults in the community. At the end of the period, young people were accepted as part of the organisation's decision-making process, and a significant shift had taken place in how young people were viewed on the estate. The organisation had developed a more positive view of young people, through learning from the experience of the project.

Encouraging entrepreneurship and autonomy

Youth work is in essence a developmental process changing over time depending on young people's expressed needs and demands; the availability of resources; and the unique combination of skills, interests and partnership opportunities in each particular setting. Workers are attracted to the work because of the opportunities it offers to create and develop, as opposed to following fixed guidelines and procedures (Millar 1995).

Much of the best practice reflects the passion and commitment of those involved. Organisations can either support or stifle this creativity through their culture, procedures and decision-making structures.

The informal, often neighbourhood-based, nature of youth work means it does not always sit easily inside broader organisational policies. Within larger organisations such as local authorities or multi-site voluntary organisations there can be tensions between corporate approaches and policies and the local experience of youth work. This tension can be felt at service or departmental level, or locally, where an individual project may come into conflict with organisational policies. Common areas of tension include rigid personnel policies designed for a stable full-time, office-based workforce; financial regulations not geared up for local externally funded projects; and unwieldy decision-making processes that preclude responsiveness to externally determined timescales.

The other side of this tension can lie with workers and young people, whose passion and commitment to the project leads them to ignore the organisational implications of their plans. The challenge for managers is to create space for innovative and creative work while retaining basic safety requirements in terms of organisational viability and legal frameworks for those participating. Some organisations, regardless of size, are better equipped than others to encourage and support entrepreneurship and innovation. A factor in this is the ability of managers and decision-makers to manage and assess risks, and develop a culture of mutual trust and co-operation between those working in the field and those who will be held accountable if it all goes wrong or disaster strikes.

Partnership friendly

Some organisations make good partners; others, perhaps because they are too concerned about their own image, too defensive or insufficiently confident to work effectively with others, do not. Most innovative youth work projects are based on partnerships: if not with other agencies, then certainly with young people and local communities. Practitioners, as a consequence of the nature of the work, tend to have good links with other agencies in their area. They would normally expect to engage with others in order to develop new initiatives that are designed to meet locally determined needs. However, their priority is often to get the work up and running as opposed to organisational concerns about profile and image. A consequence of this is that youth work agencies tend to have a low public profile, while other partners put more effort into promoting and publicising the project, often under their own 'badge'. Youth workers often experience frustration that the work they have initiated seems to have been claimed by another. Certainly, several of the managers I spoke to when preparing this chapter voiced concern that organisations which were perhaps more marginal to the success of the project often sought to claim credit for any success that was achieved. For example, a number of them recounted their frustration at the propensity of local Connexions Services to badge and claim projects staffed and managed by local youth services and voluntary organisations, but which the former had either wholly or partially funded. Successful youth work organisations need to able to work with a wide range of partners. To do so effectively they should be clear about their potential contribution to partnerships, flexible enough to work with others who may not have a full understanding of the youth work context, and sufficiently sure of their own value and worth to participate as equals in partnership with organisations that may be bigger, more broadly focused and better funded.

Responsive to change

As discussed earlier, the external context is in a constant flux. In theory, this should not prove a problem as youth work's very essence is about change and development. Youth work works with young people through transitions in their lives, enabling them to make a difference and change the communities in which they live and encouraging them to influence policies that affect their lives. However, this tolerance for, and encouragement of, change is not always reflected in the organisations that house youth work. Examples abound from both voluntary and public sector organisations that have become stuck in a particular form or range of work, while the field around them has moved on and their 'share' in youth work has been eaten away as other, more flexible organisations have taken their place.

A local authority youth centre on the edge of an urban estate with a large youth population has run a traditional programme of Junior and Senior Youth Clubs on four nights a week for the last 15 years. In that time, little has changed in either the activities offered, or in the way the building looks. Young people from the estate see it as 'boring' and dominated by one group of young people and relatively few young people now attend. In the last 5 years, external funding, channelled through voluntary organisations, has resulted in a range of new projects and activities for young people, including a motor project, peer-led drama work, residentials and detached work. The local authority is now looking at the viability of the youth centre, with a view to moving out of it altogether.

Youth work organisations need to be alert to changes affecting their area of activity and be clear enough about their core values and roles to identify opportunities to develop or consolidate areas of work. They have to demonstrate to themselves and others that they are ready to respond to new needs and initiatives and/or to show how their existing work impacts on new policy agendas. Clearly there are dilemmas in this. Youth work prides itself on being a 'values driven' area of work (Banks 1996), and needs to ensure that these values will not be compromised in new initiatives. Successful organisations must make judgements about which developments they can contribute to, and which to leave alone rather than rushing into every new initiative and losing their direction and ability to make a positive difference to young people's lives.

The 'We can do that!' syndrome

As a way out of a potentially fatal funding crisis, a medium-sized, locally based voluntary organisation adopted a 'scatter gun' approach to funding, applying for all and any pockets of money that were available. Within 2 years they had quadrupled their income, and hugely increased their range of services. However, they found that few of the funding sources were sustainable, and that several of the projects they undertook were unable to achieve the overambitious aims they had set. The organisation's ability to deliver what funders wanted was called into question.

Fortunately, the trustees and senior managers were able to spot the problem in time, and developed a clearer picture of what the organisation was good at, and where it should be focusing its energy. It has now found its niche and is able to be selective about the areas of work and funding it will bid for.

Vision, leadership and direction

The biggest difference between the findings of my earlier research and what emerged from subsequent conversations with managers is the heightened focus on the role of managers in providing vision and leadership. Previously their prime focus was on facilitating the process of youth work and enabling it to help young people make positive transitions. Now most managers have a more sophisticated analysis, recognising the greater complexity of the environment at a time when major policy changes are aimed at young people. One described a key skill for managers as 'providing an analysis of the context for youth work, matching up national and local priorities, and steering the service in the direction that enables it to have the best impact on young people'. Others talked about the need to change the 'culture' of agencies to enable them to work more effectively with other providers in a complex field. Successful managers were described by staff as 'providing a sense of direction, generating confidence both within the organisation and outside it and having a vision of where the organisation is going'.

Having a sense of the 'bigger picture' was frequently cited in more recent conversations with managers. Being able to communicate this with staff was also identified as crucial in enabling the organisation to respond to changing circumstances. One group of managers expressed frustration with a former colleague who clearly had insights into national developments, but rarely made the time to share these with the team or use them to influence organisational practice. Public and accessible explanations of the organisation's vision and aims are needed in order to enable staff, young people and partner organisations to see their role in the 'big picture'.

Leadership is a problematic concept in youth work, despite its place in youth work's historical discourse (see Harrison *et al.* 2007). Until the 1970s, youth workers were regularly referred to as 'youth leaders': in fact, even now, some youth services still refer to 'leaders-in-charge'. However, most youth workers now would be uncomfortable with the term 'youth leader'. The importance of collective action and decision-making within the youth work process can make workers suspicious of individual leaders at all levels. Leaders are assumed, often correctly, to be pushing forward their own agendas, rather than that of those who will most benefit from the work itself. In order to gain the trust and respect of youth workers leaders and managers must demonstrate that any vision and route-map they propose will be in the interests of youth work and the wider organisation.

Youth work managers should have an understanding of the occupational culture of youth work, and of the specific cultural features of the organisation they manage. Factors including the importance given within the organisation to a person-centred approach, participation in decision-making and the concept of the youth worker as an activist can work for or against organisational change. Managers must build the 'vision' for the organisation on the strengths in the existing organisational and occupational culture, while looking to change those aspects which prevent the organisation from adapting and thriving in the current climate. Managers must be able to share the vision; explain the potential benefits to staff and young people; engage staff in determining what it means for work on the ground; and they must be seen to be accountable to staff and young people, not just to the organisational hierarchy.

In my earlier research I frequently encountered confusion between 'management' and 'administration'. Managers often filled their time with paperwork, form filling and financial returns assuming this was the basis of their management role. Recent conversations, however, suggest managers have increased their confidence and capacity to identify problems and take strategic actions to enable their organisations to progress and develop their work with young people. They now see their role as to lead as well as manage the process.

Key tasks for youth work managers

Creating a clear policy framework

In order to make space for the creative work of individual youth workers and projects, managers need to ensure their organisation has a framework of policies that will help rather than hinder good practice. A well-written youth work curriculum framework, for example, makes clear what youth work aims to achieve and the methods available to undertake it. It can be used internally as a tool for training, planning and monitoring work, and externally to explain the youth work roles to young people, communities and partner organisations. Ord (2004: 50) points out that 'adopting the concept of curriculum has enabled youth work as a profession to be clearer about what youth work is, both to itself and to the outside world' (see also Ord 2007). In addition to policies defining the work the organisation needs policies to ensure staff and young people can participate in a safe, secure environment. Clear procedures for health and safety, employment practices, equal opportunities and access, handling money and record keeping are all essential in a healthy organisation. However, it is not enough for these to simply exist: those affected by them need to be familiar with their content and how to implement them.

Planning the work

Youth work has become a much more planned environment in recent years. Most organisations now produce annual plans, often as part of longer-term strategic plans. This helps ensure staff and resources are used appropriately to meet objectives set through the planning process. It also helps to identify areas where more development is needed and assists in setting priorities for individual projects and the whole organisation. Given the concerns of workers to ensure participative decision-making processes, plans are most likely to be successfully implemented if all staff are involved in putting them together and can see that their input has been recognised and included. Increasingly organisations are finding ways to involve young people in the planning process, both at the level of individual projects and wider organisation.

The planning cycle

A local authority Youth Service had several phases to its annual planning cycle:

- *Review of the extent to which plans for current year have been achieved*

- *Identification of Service Priorities, based on locally identified needs, County Council corporate objectives and Government policy objectives and targets, undertaken by Service Managers, in consultation with local and countywide youth forums and key partners (voluntary sector umbrella organisation and Connexions Service)*

- *Local Managers worked with Area Teams to produce Local Annual Plans*

- *Head of Service drew together Youth Service Annual Plan, based on local plans, adding centrally based activities*

- *Youth Service Annual Plan was discussed with County Youth Forum and approved by County Council members*

Managing staff and resources

In most youth work organisations the bulk of funding is spent on staff. The success or otherwise of projects largely depends on the skills and abilities of the staff, paid or voluntary. Staff frequently work in isolated settings, and often conduct most of their practice away from the watching eye of their manager. It is one of youth work's great strengths that it takes place where young people are, rather than where the organisation would like them to be, but this also has dangers. Workers can become isolated and feel the organisation is not interested in them or their work. Some can lose any sense of accountability to the organisation. Given these working conditions, it is essential youth workers are appropriately managed and supported.

The notion of 'supervision' as a supportive and challenging process is well embedded within youth work (Nicholls 1995; Tash 2000; Woods 2001). Many organisations are able to offer both 'management supervision', focusing on the tasks to be undertaken, and the skills and resources the worker needs to achieve them, and 'non-managerial supervision', in which workers are offered a supportive professional relationship, in which they can explore their own professional development in addition to task-related issues. It has proved to be an effective tool in creating positive working environments and many organisations include supervision within their policies for staff development. In some projects, the staffing structure, with many workers employed for only a few hours each week, it is difficult to implement individual supervision for everyone. Then it is important to ensure that other ways to enable staff to discuss concerns and developments in the work exist, for example, group evaluation sessions and team meetings.

In the past managers predominately focused attention on individual staff development processes. During the course of the last decade there has been a move towards work force planning. This takes a longer-term view of seeking to predict the skills and quantity of staff that will be required in the medium term and taking steps to prepare the organisation to meet new demands, through training existing staff and recruiting people to fill 'skills gaps'. Local Workforce Development Strategies may result in youth workers being recruited from groups not currently well represented in the field, for example, young people who move into youth work following time spent as a member of a youth project, or peer education programme (see, for example, Lloyd 2004).

Staff are not the sole resource. Managers, and often those who would not define themselves exclusively as such, are also responsible for looking after buildings, transport and development budgets. The complexity of the operational management of youth work was recognised in extended National Occupational Standards (PAULO 2002) resulting in more attention being paid to it within youth work training programmes. Perhaps more than any other professional working with young people, the youth worker needs to quickly develop their competency and confidence as a manager of other staff, resources and, of course, themselves.

Ensuring quality

Mechanisms to measure quality in youth work are relatively underdeveloped (Ofsted 2002, 2003 and 2006). Evidence of good youth work has been largely anecdotal, supported on occasion by external reviews and evaluations (see, for example, Merton 2004). Increasingly youth work organisations are putting in place quality assurance processes to help them make judgements about where good practice exists, and where action needs to be taken to improve aspects of their work. Many have now developed their own quality processes, often based on the Ofsted inspection framework (Ofsted 2003, 2005). Others have sought accreditation through external quality systems such as a 'Charter Mark'. Improving the quality of work is a key task for managers and links to all the other tasks mentioned above.

Communication

Managers are responsible for ensuring their organisations have effective systems of communication, preferably not entirely reliant on office gossip. A great many tensions and misunderstandings are created as a result of mixed messages circulating within organisations. One of the most important tasks for a manager is to ensure everyone knows at least as much as they need to know, and preferably a bit more, about events and issues that affect them. Team meetings and briefings provide opportunities to discuss key issues, while many organisations now use newsletters or e-mail communication to get information across to everyone.

Communication needs to take place with the outside world as well as within the organisation. Youth work agencies need to consider the image and information they present to partners and young people alongside their internal communication. Since the advent of Connexions companies and partnerships, the issue of 'branding' has received a much higher profile in the development of projects. Some organisations, particularly those linked to the private sector, and also some national voluntary organisations, such as Barnardos and Action for Children, have developed highly professional marketing and promotional techniques to ensure their name is in the public eye and therefore seen as a player when new initiatives are announced.

In conclusion

This chapter has sought to explore some of the 'big issues' youth work managers encounter in a complex and changing environment. It is clear that in order to benefit from the wide range of funding and partnership opportunities now available it is necessary for youth work to 'sharpen up' its management act. We cannot simply import management models from other industries, or even from other parts of the public sector. In order to manage youth work well, managers need to be aware of, and work with the occupational culture. They must adopt management strategies to fit their circumstances. Youth work operates at the informal, less structured end of the spectrum of work with young people, and it needs managers who recognise and build on its strengths rather than constrain it within an administrative straitjacket.

12 | Sustaining ourselves and our enthusiasm

Carole Pugh

> *Youth work, like many other welfare occupations, can be stressful and challenging. Variable work patterns and the demands placed on practitioners by those they work with and for can be draining and excessive. Successfully managing these pressures over time is an essential function of being a professional. Carole Pugh looks not only at the problematic nature of the work but also at the strategies practitioners make use of to effectively cope with them.*

This chapter begins by presenting an example of youth work practice. It is a composite of a number of similar sessions the author has observed over many years. What is described will sadly be familiar to many who are reading this.

Friday night in a village youth club. A club meets in a village hall and there has been ongoing conflict between the club and hall management committee for a number of years. There is no budget, the only money available is raised by subs, and as only about 10 young people attend, this is a small amount, so the equipment is old, battered and broken. As you walk into the session the young people are riding a scooter up and down the hall, the workers are having a coffee in the kitchen. There is no equipment set up as 'there's no point and it doesn't work anyway'. There is no programme running, as 'young people today don't want that kind of thing, they just want to come in and mess around'. At this point one of the hall management committee arrives, someone had broken the piano the week before, and she thinks it must be the youth club. The worker tries to defend the young people, but the hall manager sees the scooter and the marks it has made on the newly laid flooring . . . By the end of the session nothing tangible had happened, the young people had come in, hung around, messed

*about, the youth workers had done their best to contain them and then the
session finished, to be repeated the following week.*

Youth work can be a difficult job, undertaken with challenging young
people, sometimes in ill-equipped buildings, with few resources and scant
of support from the local community. There are many clubs and projects
where the workers have done their best, but lost hope. In an environment where the work is often under-funded, provision insecure and policy
threatens the principles of working informally with young people it can
be hard to remain hopeful. Hopelessness can lead to fatalism, as in the
example above, where workers are paralysed in the face of a situation
they see as unchangeable. Cynicism is another possible reaction, criticising any and all attempts at change. Others may retreat, wistfully hanging
on to memories of the 'Golden Age'. Yet the task of youth workers
relies on hopefulness; therefore we have to believe in young people's
potential and have faith that the process we engage young people in
will help release this (Halpin 2003a). To be effective we need to sustain ourselves intellectually, emotionally and physically and maintain our
enthusiasm and our hope in spite of the many things that combine to
make youth work a hard job. These include problematic working environments; job insecurity; widespread confusion within communities as
to what youth work is about; and the low status attaching to the work
(Coates 1993).

Knowing yourself

Everyone is different; there are many reasons for getting into youth
work, and perhaps even more for staying there, with different things
that inspire or frustrate. It is important to know yourself. As Blacker
and Collander-Brown, for example, show in earlier chapters, good relationships underpin all worthwhile youth work – and these cannot be
built and sustained without self-knowledge on the part of the worker.
Such knowledge also helps us to identify and understand the things
that reduce our motivation. None of us have infinite inner resources
and a loss of heart affects not only us, but also the work we do and
the people we work with. It can be hard, when things are uphill, to
stop and take time to identify the causes. But when we loose heart,
understanding why is often the first step to regaining it. Learning
to hear our 'inner youth worker', taking time and space to find, listen to and understand ourselves is important. As one educationalist
explains,

The most practical thing we can achieve in any kind of work is insight into what is happening inside us as we do it. The more familiar we are with our inner terrain, the more sure-footed our (practice) and living becomes.

(Palmer 1997: 15)

Prior to writing this chapter I interviewed five workers from a variety of backgrounds. All have experience of working in different contexts and organisations. They ranged from part-time workers, through to managers, and were aged between the early 20s and mid-40s. One was relatively new to youth work; others had been doing it for many years. All were resilient to the peaks and troughs of the work, and believed in the potential of young people. Each identified different issues and events that reduced their motivation and enthusiasm. For some frustration was the biggest demotivator, for example, identifying a need but not receiving the resources, or managerial or political backing to deal with it. Or when it felt like the structures did more to hold back than support the work. Some found it helpful to identify and work on the things they could change and influence, others to reflect back on the progress that had been made. Others struggled when they were working with particularly challenging young people. Supervision can help identify strategies for coping; sharing the problem with the wider staff team and asking for support can also be helpful. We should remember that there will always be some young people whom we struggle to reach, but also that there are many others whom we can work with and appreciate their development. It is important to take time to reflect on our work, on the relationships that are forming and progress made. Taking note of successes, moments when change is obvious or the spark in a young person becomes a flame, is important. Noticing the immediate 'little things' can help maintain momentum, while recording and evaluation can offer the opportunity to note and value progress.

There are often cycles in youth work, quiet times, which can be dull and isolating. Working alone in a community centre for 5 days in a week can be as hard as the fifth week of running a packed summer programme, when everyone is tired and frazzled. Acknowledging these cycles is important; we may need a week off after a week's outdoor education residential. We may also need to take on an additional role, or arrange more meetings and inter-agency work to get through a quiet part.

There may be some roles and tasks which we struggle with. Some workers, for example, identified finances and fund-raising as a problem, others writing reports, while some found it hard when the work focused on sports for a term. Spreading these tasks can be helpful, making sure there are also things we enjoy, asking for help and not putting off everything we dislike can lessen the problem.

Returning to, and reflecting on, our motivation can be helpful in evaluating the work we are doing and may prompt us to make decisions about the development of our work and role. Sustaining ourselves is about more than just managing and continuing the work. As youth workers the way we are, as well as what we do, creates examples for the young people we work with. Like teaching, good youth work cannot be reduced to technique; it also relies on the identity and integrity of the worker (Palmer 1998; Doyle 1999; Smith and Smith 2008). If we are to support young people in their learning and growing, we too must continue to learn and grow ourselves. We must attend to the ideals, morals and values that guide our understanding of what makes for human flourishing (Jeffs and Smith 1990).

Maintaining intellectual and emotional development

In the daily round, too often reading material does not move beyond memos and letters, fund-raising applications and minutes of meetings. Conversations and thinking are frequently limited to the details and complexities of planning, running and troubleshooting. Training overwhelmingly focuses on policy updates and skills acquisition. Opportunities to reflect on the direction of our work, the way this interacts with our ideas of what we hope to achieve may present themselves through annual review processes, or supervision, but equally they may be bumped off the bottom of the list by the need to respond to an altered funding agenda or staff shortages.

If we hope to remain engaged, reflective and effective practitioners it is important to make space for our continued development. Or as Brew (1943) argues, if we are bored with ourselves, we are likely to be boring to the young people we work with. In order to remain interesting and engaging we need to continually develop social, cultural and intellectual interests that can enhance the quality of work we do. Jeffs and Smith (2005: 111–112) identify six basic modes of work: being around, being there, working with individuals and groups, doing projects, doing admin and, central to these, reflecting on practice. Eraut (1994: 156) argues that reflection lies at the heart of taking responsibility for our continuing development and ongoing evaluation of practice. Indeed, failing to undertake this is irresponsible. All this requires time. However, it should not be added to the never-ending list of things we want to do but rarely, if ever, get around to. This reduces motivation. It needs to be built into the way we work. There will be times when it is a low priority, but equally, there should be some times when it is not.

Making time to read material beyond the daily round can provide access to a wider range of ideas and ways of working. It can enable us to locate our work as part of a broader picture which can encourage and inspire. Visiting other agencies and projects, and meeting others can also give new insights and perspectives. Accessing educational opportunities beyond practical issues can support development. Giving ourselves a reason to do this can help ensure it does not also fall of the bottom of the list: agree to run a training course, prepare a discussion paper, develop a new project, create a resource or undertake a new role that will stretch us.

Another component of developing learning and reflection, and receiving support and feedback relies on creating a network of people who understand and are equally committed. Growing interest in learning organisations during the last decade highlighted the importance of informal networks and groupings in creating environments where people are able to share knowledge and nurture creative thinking (Senge 1990). Lave and Wenger (1991) have also identified a model of 'situated learning' where members learn through the process of engaging with a 'community of practice' (Wenger 1998, 2005). This brings them together by engaging in and learning through common activities. Members develop relationships over time and also gather and develop resources such as tools, documents, ideas and shared understandings.

Joining a 'community of practice', engaging with people who inspire, encourage, challenge, support and stimulate, can develop learning for individuals and also the organisations they are part of. Finding or creating such a group is not easy; opportunities to meet must be actively sought and defended. Opportunities to extend conversations started at conferences or training events with workers from other organisations or areas should be seized. It is not only physical meetings that offer opportunities; phone calls, e-mail and the Internet can support 'virtual communities of practice'. For example, the informal education site www.infed.org. and the Federation for Detached Youth Workers forums/communities can be invaluable as a means of linking up with others to share ideas and insights. Time must be set aside to engage in the sort of conversation where ideas and broader issues are explored; it is easy in a pressured practice environment to only look at ways of meeting new targets and performance indicators rather than considering the wider issues of the impact this changing philosophy of managing the work may actually be having on its character. It is important to create spaces and environments where you are encouraged to develop questions and explore alternative routes. Creating a 'steering group' for a particular project or piece of work; holding networking or forum meetings for workers in a related area; participating in a web forum; or organizing 'out of work' gatherings are feasible strategies for doing this.

Management

It is important to know and understand our line management structure and accountability procedures. Promoting good practice requires that managers create environments that support and stimulate staff. Most workplaces have some systems for supervision, staff training, appraisal and review. While they are often not ideal, indeed a review of Ofsted reports reveals that less than a quarter of services examined have satisfactory supervision practices (Jenkinson 2002), they can offer structures from which we may benefit.

Supervision is a vital part of practice, and needs to be rooted in a commitment to staff development, training and support (Christian and Kitto 1987; Tash 2000; Woods 2001). It is a professional tool and not merely a management system for monitoring and control. Within youth work there are two main forms of supervision: managerial supervision, which is undertaken by your line manager, and non-managerial (or professional) supervision, provided by someone external to the organisation. These distinctions are often characterised by managerial supervision's focus on the interest of the organisation, and non-managerial supervision's focus on the development of the worker. However, non-managerial supervisors also have a responsibility to ensure that practice meets basic minimum standards, in order to protect the young people with whom we work (Smith 2005). Supervision should be a learning opportunity for both participants and needs to be undertaken at regular intervals in a private space, to have been prepared for (by both parties) and to be undertaken in a spirit of openness (Nicholls 1999). Supervision should embrace addressing issues of accountability and administration by promoting and maintaining good standards of work and ensuring the understanding and application of policies. This should be balanced with providing opportunities for professional development and education as well as offering support (Hargreaves 2002; Kadushin and Harness 2002; Thompson 2007). There can be tensions between these. The wrong balance, for example where there is an overemphasis on accountability, may lead to a situation where workers feel unable to share problems or openly discuss their practice. Equally undue focus on personal support can lead to workers feeling the reason they are struggling results from their personal inadequacy, rather than the structures within which they operate. It is important we take some responsibility for using and getting the most out of supervision structures by preparing for sessions, and thinking about the issues we want to discuss, the support we would like and what we wish to get out of the process. If we are not offered supervision or it is inadequate, it is our professional responsibility to do something about it.

Many of the workers I spoke to found additional support networks by talking with colleagues and friends, sharing ideas and frustrations. Ingram and Harris (2001: 86) identify six areas of useful support:

- Somewhere to go for acceptance;
- Somewhere that you can systematically review the work;
- Somewhere that ideas can be generated;
- Somewhere that problems can be solved;
- Somewhere to be with others in similar roles;
- Somewhere to go to find information.

Reflecting on your needs in these terms, at times when you are struggling, and identifying someone who can help you meet these can provide invaluable support. Different people and teams will probably provide for these needs at different times. Informal support mechanisms can provide valuable input but often rely on sensitive use and reciprocity, awareness of colleagues' situations and a willingness to offer reciprocal support when appropriate.

Boundaries and burnout

Many of those interviewed identified tiredness as a key factor in reduced motivation. There is often a tendency for workers to do more than their required hours. Some workers see youth work as both a job and a hobby and make a conscious decision to undertake extra 'voluntary' hours; others wish to stick to their contracted hours but find they struggle to do all that is expected of them in the allotted time (Ingram and Harris 2001). Extra commitment needs to be noted and valued; however, it can also create pressure on others who do not put in as many hours. Individuals cannot be expected to undertake additional, 'voluntary', work merely because others opt to do so.

Managing time is an important skill and requires attention. It's vital to be aware of the tasks we have to get done, to estimate how long they will take and to prioritise them. If there is insufficient time, we need to make decisions about how we handle this. Can we leave a task until later, or ask someone else to do it? Do we need to talk to our line manager about the roles we have undertaken and look to reducing them? Can we work longer in the next few weeks and take time off in lieu next month when it is quieter? Working under pressure can fuel an extra sense of purpose but if there is no end point and we constantly feel we should be working this cannot be sustained. We, as well as our line managers, have a responsibility to manage our time. This includes monitoring workloads, seeking support from colleagues and line managers as appropriate and, perhaps above all else, asking what can young people be doing for themselves. It is all too easy to sideline young people, to fall into providing for them rather than viewing them as active participants.

The tendency for the work to be organised in split sessions can lead to workers not taking clear 'time off'. The actual hours worked in a day may not be excessive, but they can easily be spread between 9 AM and 9 PM with little free time in between. Combining different part-time jobs creates similar tensions. Pressure to be flexible and be available for the 'one-off' Monday night training is common. This can leave workers feeling like they have 'no life outside work'. It is important to learn to maintain boundaries. Blocking out sections in our diaries when we are 'not available' and protecting these is crucial. Having regular times off during the week when we are committed to being somewhere other than work can help: a regular pub quiz, swimming session, cricket team commitment or night in with our family.

Sometimes the reason you find yourself struggling is that you are trying to 'carry' another team member. While it is important to offer practical and emotional support to other members of the team if they are struggling, it is also essential to recognise there are limits to this. Sometimes the need for 'a little extra support' extends into propping up a worker who does not have the necessary skills or motivation to effectively undertake their role. Youth workers are used to encouraging and supporting young people, providing second and third chances as they learn through their experiences; this tolerance is also often applied to workers. In an environment where it is hard to recruit people to post, the pressure to tolerate lower standards of practice can increase. However, when a colleague consistently neglects to turn up on time – or doesn't turn up at all; doesn't do the preparation they said they would; or fails to engage with young people there comes a time when their right to additional support runs out. In these situations motivation can be even harder to maintain when everyone in the team begins to feel the pressure and it can lead to a cumulative sense of hopelessness and lack of purpose, as in the club described at the beginning of the chapter.

Most organisations have procedures for dealing with poor practice; it is important you are familiar with these. Usually they begin with offering additional support and training to a worker, along with closer supervision and monitoring. If this fails to resolve the problem there are 'capability' or 'disciplinary' mechanisms that seek to investigate poor practice and can lead, in the worst cases, to dismissal. As a worker you may feel uncomfortable challenging poor practice or ensuring your line manager is aware of the situation. You will need to reflect on the situation and decide personally when you feel the line between the need for extra support and an inability or unwillingness to effectively undertake a role has been crossed. While we have a duty to support our colleagues we also have a duty to the young people we work with to provide a high quality of service, and where a worker is consistently not meeting minimum standards we have a professional obligation to take some action. Covering for a colleague who engages in bad practice, for example, allowing young people to drink in the building, can undermine the work of the rest of the team as well as the reputation of other youth workers in the area. Flagging this up will be uncomfortable but may enable the worker to ask for the extra training or support they need. It may also lead to 'capability' or 'disciplinary' procedures, which, although painful in the short term, usually leads to change. Keeping quiet will rarely enable the situation to be resolved.

When you've had enough, stop, and try something else . . .

There are times in jobs when maintaining motivation and enthusiasm becomes very difficult. This can be because the pressure of the work is too much, or because it has become repetitive and predictable and lost its challenge. Achieving change can be tiring, especially if we are trying to keep a project going. There are times when we have to make decisions about carrying on, or re-directing our energy to somewhere else. One worker spoke of struggling to 'just hold onto the strings'. Alternatively it may be that we feel we have given and gained all we can from a job. One worker interviewed spoke of 'growing out of a job'; they were able to identify their enthusiasm for the project was waning, as it no longer presented the challenges they once thrived on. The option to change jobs and work in a new environment, with different people and challenges, can be vital in sustaining ourselves.

Equally others gain the most satisfaction from staying in a project in the long term. Being able to take a longer view and identify the changes that they had contributed to over a number of years, or even decades, provides them with the impetus and motivation they require to sustain themselves. Remaining in post does not mean you cannot make changes to your routine or how you approach the work; for example, it may be possible to alter your role to incorporate new challenges and remove aspects you are bored with. Sometimes considering alternative posts can provide you with insight into what it is about your current role that is weighing you down and give you the impetus to try to change it. Ultimately only you can make the decision to stay or go; therefore, knowing yourself is vital in considering these issues.

And finally remaining hopeful

All the workers interviewed could still identify positive reasons for why they choose to do the job. There are good grounds to remain hopeful and motivated: when policy changes, when a new youth centre opened, when young people attend and participate in a community meeting or when, 5 years later, we bump into a young man who still has, and values, a video of an arts project he did. As one worker explained:

> If you look, you can actually see the tangible benefits from the impact of your work, a young person making a decision, becoming more involved, developing. It's not only about working towards a wider, more universal or intangible 'good', but also actually seeing the small differences that you made.

Remaining hopeful is central to maintaining motivation. Imagining the impact a new piece of provision could have on an estate or the way a young woman could learn to take control of her life and fulfil her potential provides us with the impetus for hope. These 'images of alternative futures' (Halpin 2003a) can provide an antidote to burnout, fatalism and frustration. Belief in the potential inherent in the young people we work with alongside a faith in the capacity of the youth work process to draw this out can motivate us. We can use examples of inadequate practice as illustrations and springboards to think about change. By holding on to the reasons we undertake the work, the opportunities for development, change and growth; and finding, creating and using systems for prompting reflection, development and gaining support we can sustain our enthusiasm. Youth work, like any other job, can be uphill sometimes. But I think it's worth it. Just consider how things are, or might be, and compare this vignette with the one that appeared on the first page of this chapter.

> *Meanwhile in a village nearby, the workers have arrived 15 minutes early to move 200 chairs from one part of the hall so that a table tennis table can be put up. As the club opens around 60 young people come in. The first ones in help finish off setting up. On the door the workers chat with the young people, reminding them of things that are going on. One group has raised funds for a trip; they need to think about organising a mini bus. There is a members, committee meeting to be organised, and nominations and election of a new committee to be thought about. Half way through the*

session a group of 19-year-olds arrive, they are on their way in to town to go out drinking. One is just back from university and wanted to pop in to let the youth worker know how it was all going. Towards the end of the session the workers encourage the young people to start closing up. The chairs are moved back, the hall swept, and the building closed up until the following week.

13 | Monitoring and evaluating youth work

John Rose

As the amount of youth work sponsored by local and central government has grown so we have seen an increase in the extent to which the practice of workers and performance of agencies has been monitored and evaluated by funders. John Rose looks at the implications this has for practice and the benefits and problems arising from a heightened increase in the monitoring and evaluation of youth work.

Most funders monitor and evaluate youth work using an '*accountability model*'. This model is being pushed forward by a continuing political agenda that prioritises 'economy, effectiveness and quality'. It is an ideology underpinned by systems which allocate financial resources based on an ability to demonstrate through the attainment of measurable outcomes that the specified requirements are met. Consequently, additional bidding, monitoring and evaluation processes have been introduced to ensure that funders, often the government, are more able to control 'delivery'.

This approach has also become the accepted way of judging young people's learning. Driven by the examination culture schools have refined their structures, management styles, teaching methods, monitoring and evaluation systems in an attempt to ensure young people secure ever-improving examination results (Griffith 2000). School-based monitoring systems are in use to manage the effective knowledge acquisition of young people. These are concerned to keep a continuous record of the incremental learning of pupils through their involvement in standardised individual testing. The overall evaluation of the process as a means of judging school effectiveness is measured against the attainment of the stipulated outcomes. The inability of individual schools to attain the outcomes leads to the school being publicly labelled as 'failing' or 'failed'. This approach has also had a profound effect upon youth work. Current policy and practice have become underpinned by the belief that the primary outcome measure of educational achievement is examination results.

Youth work and the new managerialism

The challenges faced by youth workers within this new environment appear to be of little concern or interest to governments. The political position is unambiguous. To secure government support workers have to identify the outcomes of their interventions in relation to their contribution to the delivery of the government's economic and social agenda. As a consequence many, perhaps most, youth workers are asked to quantify how they contribute to, for example:

- Increasing the numbers of young people staying in, or returning to education.
- Preparing young people for the world of work.
- Reducing crime and anti-social behaviour.
- Improving health.
- Raising levels of political involvement.

If agencies fail to do this on time and to a specified standard they will be punished. Youth services and agencies are becoming more like other 'human service' organisations driven by the threat of withdrawal of funding, faced with enhanced competition, increased bureaucracy and external inspections.

To survive, many youth workers and agencies have developed new evaluation and monitoring systems. Some have sought to make them more relevant to what they see as the guiding principles of youth work. Many hold that from such principles a set of values can be agreed which help determine ways of working with young people that respect basic human rights, their uniqueness as individuals, the right to self-determination and the educational and social importance of choice, freedom, responsibility and justice (Banks 1999). Youth workers like others operating in social welfare organisations need to develop 'through the prism of their own specialism' (Drakeford 1998) discrete modes of evaluation and monitoring.

What do youth services and agencies need to do?

Youth workers should not automatically reject or avoid the idea of monitoring and evaluation as a process. Rather, there should be recognition of their potential contribution to the development of practice and as a means of consolidating youth work. Those involved in the monitoring and evaluation debate should be exploring new developments in the search for more appropriate methods of valuing the learning involved as a result of young people's engagement with youth work. At the same time youth services and agencies should also be giving consideration to a small number of issues each of which have, if left unresolved, the potential to distort how the work is monitored and evaluated.

First, we need to address the confusion within youth work regarding the relationship between purpose, principles, values and ethics. This is not to suggest there is a general lack of knowledge about these issues, which are well documented in a range of publications (NYA 2000; WYA 2002). It is more about recognising the difficulties associated with the embedded collective understanding of the 'essence' of youth work and the difficulties related to agreed definitions of as to what youth work '**does**', how it '**does it**' and what '**results**' are planned and achieved. Practitioners found that achieving this is more difficult because of the conflicts they encounter between a professional code, which advocates attention to the expressed needs of individuals and groups, and bureaucratic pressure for increased efficiency and compliance to predetermined outcomes. This conflict is constantly exacerbated by the need for workers to maintain their levels of professional knowledge in a rapidly changing practice environment, which often challenges their philosophical and knowledge base. This can result in a situation where patterns of task and knowledge are inherently unstable (Schön 1983).

Second, there is a historic difficulty in defining and measuring the outcomes of youth work practice. The work of youth services is increasingly driven by a belief that effective programmes will develop in young people a wide range of what are described as 'soft skills' or 'enhanced emotional intelligence'. These include fostering attributes and skills such as an ability to communicate, work in teams, solve problems, and develop self-esteem or display 'initiative'. The monitoring and evaluation of the extent to which youth work interventions sponsor the acquisition of these characteristics is difficult if not impossible. For example, workers lack access both to the point young people have reached prior to intervention and the extent to which other, parallel, learning experiences contribute to change. As a consequence, there is no credible 'scale' able to measure the 'distance travelled by young people'. Even if it were possible to develop the tools to measure progress, a problem would remain. The philosophical position of much youth work has located the ownership and assessment of learning with young people. This requires an approach that recognises the intrinsic value of learning managed through the development of the skills of action and reflection (Freire 1972). However, such approaches have little credibility within an environment that perceives monitoring and evaluation as management tools whose primary function is to ensure that set objectives are achieved within the cost calculations imposed by policy makers.

Third, what appears to have happened, and what seems to be continuing to happen, is the plagiarising of models more appropriate to other areas of work including formal school- and college-based education. The consequence of this is all too obvious. There is a growing trend to involve young people in a range of activities that lend themselves to monitoring and evaluation processes linked to outcomes measured by external sources. Open College Network (OCNs), National Vocational Qualifications (NVQs), Youth Achievement Awards, Award Scheme Development and Accreditation Network (ASDANs) and their like are proliferating within a new youth work environment driven by political dogma. We need to step back from this before it is too late and recognition of the special contribution of youth work is lost within the new landscape of managerialism and accountability.

What do youth workers need to do?

Within this context youth workers need to undertake a number of tasks. In particular they must:

- Identify the various strands of monitoring and evaluation that are to be found in a complex organisation such as youth and children's services;
- Identify appropriate methods of monitoring and evaluation that reflect the wide range of accountabilities relevant to the responsibilities of the youth services and agencies;
- Recognise that monitoring and evaluation of the outcomes of their work with young people should reflect the purpose, principles and values of their work, which places ownership of the process in the hands of young people;
- Recognise that this concept is almost always alien to government, funding bodies and other professional organisations and most importantly – because of their previous experiences – to young people themselves.

Those working within youth and children's services should know the concept of monitoring as a system employing a variety of tools that warn, check, control or keep a continuous record of things that need to be known. The same can also be said about the idea of *evaluation*, which is a process to judge or assess the worth of a particular act or product. The rules of monitoring and evaluation are also easy to locate, as are the theoretical styles for conducting them. It is also relatively easy to identify the reasons why monitoring and evaluation are useful organisational tools.

An examination of the characteristics of monitoring and evaluation describes a process dependent on:

- A clear understanding of the purpose/principles/values/ethics of the setting being monitored and evaluated;
- Deciding the purpose of the monitoring and evaluation process;
- Agreeing the style of monitoring and evaluation to be adopted;
- Describing the intended outcomes of the project;
- Designing monitoring and evaluation systems that reflect the context within which they are to be used;
- Describing the process to be used (this should be accordant with the purpose and the style of approach to be adopted, which would be constructed to be compatible with agreed principles, values and ethics);
- Identifying the roles and responsibilities of those involved in the setting being monitored and evaluated;
- Agreeing benchmarks in the development of the project;
- Agreeing the types of evidence to be used to measure that objectives have been met;
- Determining reasons for success or failure as measured against achieving intended outcomes;
- Reflection and review.

Within this framework youth workers need to recognise at least three different strands of monitoring and evaluation within youth work and understand their relative importance to its young people-first approach. These strands are related to measuring:

- organisation criteria;
- the role and functions of the youth worker;
- the learning of young people who come into contact with youth work agencies and services.

The first strand is about monitoring and evaluating the range of management responsibilities relevant to the roles and responsibilities of the youth worker, including finance, personnel, risk assessment, health and safety and child protection. Guidance on how these and other elements are monitored and evaluated is normally contained within the standing orders of most local authorities and voluntary organisations. These often require the youth worker to follow agreed procedures, which meet audit arrangements, relevant legislation and agreed quality standards. The collection of this type of data generally relies on quantitative methods of collection involving the service manager, youth worker, young people and others from outside of the organisation. This type of information is often supplemented by the collection of other quantifiable data sometimes requested by employing organisations but often developed as an aid to individual workers to improve practice. It often includes:

- The overall attendance levels and attendance patterns of individuals;
- The length of time particular young people have been in contact with the agency or service;
- The age and gender of those attending;
- A record of the types of activities undertaken;
- A record of qualifications and attainments as a result of involvement in the agency's or service's activities.

The second strand is related to monitoring and evaluating the effectiveness of the youth worker measured against how work with young people is carried out in a way that reflects the agreed purpose, principles, values and ethics of the work. The targets for measuring these are often contained within a range of organisational documents including, for example, Strategic and Operational Plans; policy documents; job descriptions; time sheets; and recording sheets. Governments also set benchmarks which impact directly on the roles and functions of the youth worker and these too need systems of monitoring and evaluating to check that the effectiveness of services can be measured. These government benchmarks in more recent times have often been focused on reducing what are described by Huskins (2001) as the dangerous behaviour of young people. Included in this description are truancy and school exclusion, drug misuse, risky sexual behaviour, and crime and anti-social behaviour. This agenda normally uses utilitarian methods of monitoring and evaluation including quantifiable evidence to suggest, for example, that school truancy and school exclusion, criminal activities and anti-social behaviour by the young had been reduced as a result of youth work interventions. From this perspective the things that should be known to those within youth work – obtained from appropriate monitoring and evaluation systems – are influenced by a set of general principles, which describe young people as deficient and in need of rehabilitation.

If youth workers follow the government agenda, however, there will be a need to recognise what Young (2006: 2) describes as the moral philosophy of youth work: a position concerned to 'enable and support young people to ask and answer the central question of self – what sort of person am I? What kind of relationship do I want to have with myself and others? What kind of society do I want to live in?' From this starting point the things that need to be known by those within the work change fundamentally, as does the ownership of what needs to be known. The first model suggests that what needs to be known, needs to be known by those in positions of power, which generally means the adult youth worker on behalf of a greater authority. The second model takes a completely different view in that the position is driven by a young person-first approach, which recognises that ownership of what needs to be known is firmly in the control of the **individual** young person.

As a result of the greater involvement of government this young person-first approach presents a significant challenge regarding how the youth worker monitors and evaluates their work within the current political environment. This challenge is caused primarily by the entrenched view of government – sometimes aided by those within youth services – that young people are a homogeneous group capable of being altered as a consequence of establishment reform. Changes to the school system, increases to the range of further and higher education opportunities, new criminal justice arrangements, work experience and training schemes are all too often seen as ways of ensuring the government's agenda is being met – often at the expense of individuals. This needs to be challenged by those within youth work, underpinned as it is by the particular moral philosophy described previously. There is a need to move more closely to a position where young people during their involvement with youth workers are recognised as individuals requiring access to a range of strategies able to equip them to make sense of their own life. For services and agencies this is a process concerned to give young people ownership of the decisions that affect them. The outcome of such an approach is the development in young people of skills that enable them to reflect on their actions, which in turn leads to more positive personal decisions and more appropriate actions. The challenge is great but so are the possible outcomes for young people, the communities within which they live and to the economic and social agenda of government. These outcomes will not only be measured by statistics related to increases in formal educational attainment or reductions in crime and anti-social behaviour. They will also be measured by the general contribution young people make to society through an enhanced understanding of the link between their individual **rights** and associated **responsibilities** as citizens.

For services and agencies driven by a philosophically moral perspective the key to developing awareness and understanding of the personal rights and responsibilities by young people is the idea of 'appropriate education' with its potential to:

- Enable young people to act well and to seek excellence within the social practices in which they engage – (communication, team working and problem solving);
- Enable young people to make reasonable choices;
- Enable young people to develop a consistent character;
- Enable young people to determine for themselves the characteristics of a life worth living.

The nature of and the availability of this *appropriate education* within the community context has been largely disregarded by governments who continue to generally ignore the importance of a style of learning which does not use a mechanistic system of measurement. As a consequence, current thinking by decision-makers has been too concerned to place the education and learning of young people as the almost exclusive remit of formal school-based education. Delivering this responsibility has, however, become a near impossible task for schools, affected as they are by a changing, complex society. Rowan Williams, the Archbishop of Canterbury, recognised this during his 2002 Dimbleby Lecture by arguing that the attainment of appropriate education (skills, knowledge and attitude) by young people is being diminished because the institutions that have historically helped many of them shape their lives are not always available. Consequently, too many young people are excluded from family continuity, access to conventional religious practice or involvement in shared public activity. For many young people, particularly those faced with issues of multiple deprivation, work and relationships have become increasingly transient. Within this unstable environment formal school-based education is, in the opinion of the Archbishop, fighting a losing battle to 'sustain a tradition on behalf of the whole community, an accepted set of perspectives on human priorities and relationships, a feel for the conventions of life'.

The development of personal qualities obtained as a result of appropriate education, therefore, needs to take a more radical approach through a more equitable partnership between school- and community-based education and learning, and between formal and non-formal approaches.

From this philosophical standpoint, education and learning opportunities can be and are created in the community, which involves many young people who have – and who have not – been successful within the school system. Learning opportunities through, for example, sport, art, music, drama, outdoor activities, international travel, conservation and involvement in community activities are available to many young people through their contact with a wide range of community-based youth work organisations.

The third strand is concerned with the monitoring and evaluation of the achievements of young people as a result of their involvement with youth services and agencies. This is most important. It should be recognised that the previous two strands of monitoring and evaluation have as their single purpose the delivery of a service capable of contributing to the personal and social development of young people. This third area of monitoring and evaluation is a complex process but critical as a means of ensuring the measurement of the outcomes of that involvement are considered in a way that reflects organisational purpose, principles, values and ethics. This will require the further refinement and use of a range of monitoring and evaluation tools more appropriate to the nature of youth work. Two of these I believe are core and can be supplemented by a number of other tools in a way that enhances the validity and reliability of the information being obtained.

The first tool is self-assessment which recognises that the monitoring and evaluation of a young person's experiences through their involvement with youth work is firmly under their individual control. As stated previously, a frequently asked question of services is about how they measure the distance travelled by young people through involvement in their activities. Youth workers must be able to develop appropriate processes that enable us to reply with confidence that this is a question more appropriately answered by young people themselves. The support for young people to develop the skills to achieve this is one of the greatest challenges. Persuading those in power that it is a credible process with important self-determined outcomes will be another.

A second tool is youth worker observation, reflection and recording. The use of the youth worker as a monitoring and evaluation tool fits comfortably within the philosophically moral position described previously, provided it is carried out in a way that reflects the principles, values and ethics of the organisation. This process of observation, reflection and recording is critically linked to the quality of the relationship between the youth worker and young person. Both the processes of observation and reflection and subsequent recording should be concerned with providing opportunities to individuals and groups through appropriate education.

It is from this position that a contribution to identifying the things that need to be known by those within the work can be obtained. Supporting the information obtained through self-assessment by young people and the observation, reflection and recordings of the youth worker are a range of other tools including, for example, the use of appropriate formal accreditation systems and the use of statistical evidence. The importance of this approach is the use made of multiple methods of monitoring and evaluation which are used in combination to provide evidence about the things that need to be known by young people as a result of their involvement with youth work agencies and services.

How can we go forward?

The strength of the youth work agency is its educational role which is the priority for the various UK governments in their attempts to successfully achieve an economic and social regeneration agenda. It can be argued, however, that this role is simultaneously its weakness because of the way government policy is driving a formal examination process.

To ensure young people benefit from a broader education and learning opportunities both within school and the community, youth services and agencies need to prove themselves, through the use of appropriate mechanisms, as effective organisations. However, in doing so they must guard against being drawn into adopting only the control mechanisms employed by formal school-based education and learning.

To provide the most appropriate education and learning opportunities for young people agencies and services need to make available evidence to prove the 'examination culture' is inappropriate at a number of different levels – particularly the way it attempts to establish links between academic attainment and economic success. This has been challenged for a number of reasons. First because it is seen to fail to develop in young people the ability to effectively transfer formal educational experiences into other areas of their lives, including work and leisure. Second because this culture fails to encourage wider problem-solving and continuing learning. Arguments are also available to suggest that the measurement of formal levels of education is inappropriate, as a standard of attainment, because of its failure to measure real levels of education. This real level, it is claimed, should include education and learning obtained from outside of the institutionalised and accredited arena and can be located, as a non-formal learning process, within the wider community of family, friends, work and leisure.

What then is the role of youth services and agencies with their commitment to informal and non-formal community-based education and learning? Are they able to make a contribution to the education and learning of young people complementary to that being offered through the formal school-based system? Are they able to clearly articulate the process of education and learning it undertakes with young people? Are they able to determine the outcomes of its work with young people? Are they able to be seen as effective contributors to the government's agenda while at the same time maintaining their unique role in the lives of young people? Should they be concerned to introduce procedures and different measuring instruments from those already in use in the formal education sector?

The current political climate has set new challenges. It questions the ability of youth work agencies to meet the needs of young people and stresses the requirements of government around the attainment of specific outcomes. Youth workers need to go back to the work of educators such as Illich (1971) and Freire (1972), educators who challenge the effectiveness of formal education in isolation by offering a broader perspective about the values of non-formal learning. They also argue that formal learning systems offer a certain type of arrangement for learning which may not suit the needs of many in society, implying that the formal context for learning offers some an opportunity for learning but not all. To overcome these failings Illich, for example, suggests that systems could be developed to 'provide the learner with new links to the world instead of continuing to funnel all educational programmes through the teacher' (1971: 73). If this approach is to be adopted more widely and its value recognised as a complementary form of education to that found in formal school-based education, alternative methods of monitoring and evaluation, involving young people as key participants, will need to be used. Rather than coaching young people to pass examinations processes will need to be further refined in order to develop in young people a critical consciousness arrived at through a process of reflection and action. It will be a system prepared not only to place the ownership of learning in the hands of the learner but also to place its valuing.

In conclusion

To influence the education debate the services and agencies urgently need to promote youth work's non-formal community-based approach. It results in education and learning opportunities being made available in a wide range of settings. This includes working with young people in specialist clubs, at centres for curriculum specialities such as art, theatre, outdoor activities, or sport, on the streets or in other areas where they meet. Non-formal education and learning involves the voluntary commitment and active participation of young people who are involved in assessing need, designing learning experiences, locating resources and evaluating learning. This action and subsequent reflection is made possible as a result of a maturing process within which individual self-concept moves from dependency to inter-dependency assisted by an expanding bank of experience that becomes useful as a learning resource. Its approach is driven by a philosophical position underpinned by two implicit principles.

● Knowledge is assumed to be actively constructed by the learner not passively received from the environment;
● Learning is an interactive process of interpretation, integration and transformation of one's experiential world.

The creation of this environment is made possible through the use of working methods based on principles of participation and empowerment and the use of a range of methods arrived at as a result of mutual agreement between practitioners and young people. This basis of negotiation and contract serves as the foundation for a particular style of *learning* within which young people can make informed decisions about the direction of their lives for themselves. It is not a position that easily lends itself to a process of monitoring and evaluation of the style required by a government concerned with the attainment of measurable targets. Youth services and agencies need to challenge this position with their growing emphasis upon 'accreditation' measured by methodological and mechanistic methods. To do this effectively they will need to devise and promote new systems that both fit the culture of youth work and convince government and other funding sources of their reliability and validity.

Conclusion

Everything before us exists in the ideal world. The future is a blank and dreary void, like sleep or death, till the imagination brooding over it with wings outspread, impregnates it with life and motion. The forms and colours it assumes are but pictures reflected on the eye of fancy, the unreal mockeries of future events. The solid fabric of time and nature moves on, but the future always flies before it.

William Hazlitt

All times are times of transition. Although it is possible to identify continuities within youth work, for example the focus on conversation and relationships, the need for relevance and the centrality of voluntary affiliation, social and political changes have unceasingly restructured the work since its beginnings in the early years of industrialisation. Unending adaptation will be a feature of practice in the decades to come, just as in the past. As society changes and the experiences of young people simultaneously alter, youth work must re-order itself to avoid marginalisation and irrelevance. For the informal educational core to endure it is always necessary for the periphery to be in a permanent state of flux.

Recent government policy documents, as we noted on Chapter 1, have barely discussed youth work as an entity or option. Driven forward by a fear of being perceived as soft on crime, soft on young thugs, soft on anti-social behaviour (a Frankenstein monster of their own making) and a need to achieve self-imposed educational targets based upon narrow academic and behavioural criterion, governments in Britain lost what little faith they may have once had in the value of youth work and informal education. A social policy agenda, set with one eye upon securing the approval of the *Daily Mail*'s editor and that paper's assumed readership, has no room for the seemingly vague outcomes promised by traditional models of youth work. Indeed, at various times ministers have articulated their impatience with both youth work and informal education, and their doubts as to the worth of both of them. Therefore, in the short run it is probably beneficial for youth work to slip the leash of direct state funding where it can. Certainly, there is not much likelihood that it will for the time being prosper as part of the statutory welfare sector. The historical relationship based upon mutuality and collaboration between the state and voluntary sector going back to the early years of the Second World War has ended. In this era of commissioning, the state will look to fund work with young people but not youth work. The raising of the school-leaving age to 18, the growth of mass higher education and demographic shifts that work to further marginalise young people in relation to the political agenda all conspire to make survival less rather than more likely.

What is happening to state-sponsored youth work is not unprecedented. It has been pre-figured by the destruction of adult liberal education, which in the 'academic year' 2007–2008 alone lost 1,500,000 students (Hook 2008). The survival of both youth work and liberal adult education now primarily depends on the voluntary sector, autonomous groupings and those institutions receiving state monies such as schools that have been able to carve out some discretion. However, whatever its strengths in terms of the capacity to relate to organic communities and foster the development of innovative modes of practice, the voluntary sector ultimately cannot deliver in relation to social justice and the formation of a more egalitarian and fairer society. Only a system of collective invention based on a fair and equitable tax system will achieve that end (Wilkinson and Pickett 2009: 215–265). As Moore (1995) suggests, in order to introduce the required radical shift in the loci of public services, positive support is needed not merely from those likely to directly benefit, the 'clients or direct consumers', but from the wider community or citizens. To secure this there needs to be public engagement and the sort of democratic deliberation that encourages individuals and communities to adopt an informed and socially aware perspective regarding the benefits of a welfare or social intervention. In lieu of that happening it is inevitable that the structures created to service a different era will fall apart.

All is not lost. We can never go back but we can re-build and rescue what is worthwhile if we so desire. The implications of our analysis are fairly clear. Workers and managers, by deepening their appreciation of youth work, being open to the call of community and having an eye for opportunity, can push boundaries. They can develop more relational and open forms of work with young people. The space to do this varies with the setting and with how far agencies have been pulled into practice that is concerned with monitoring, management and the achievement of centrally defined outcomes in individuals. Individuals can also choose not to work in organisations that seek to act on (rather than with) young people and undermine their privacy. However, there is only so much that individual workers and managers can do. They need to join with others to engineer more substantial change. This might take the form of small groups or teams of workers developing new initiatives or attempting to safeguard existing groups, projects and clubs that offer sanctuary, relationship and hope to young people. Hopefully, more will choose to take their place in civil society – by looking for the opportunity to develop work within local groups and organisations, and by organising through unions, professional groupings and the movements that still play a significant part in youth work. There is a long agenda for action here including:

- Campaigning for work rooted in local communities, civil society and democratic endeavour;
- Opposing mechanisms and approaches that demean children and young people and subject them to unwarranted surveillance and control;
- Revealing the bankruptcy of the delivery model of social provision and its accompanying machinery – commissioning, service level agreements and the like;
- Arguing for funding and working arrangements that move beyond a narrow, outcome focus.

These are all parts of the larger challenge to cultivate the civic and democratic renewal necessary so that people may better share in the common life. But we can only start where we are and ultimately put our trust in relationship, conversation and association. If we do then all sorts of things are possible for, as Hazlitt assures us, the 'future flies before' and we alone 'can impregnate it with life'.

References

Ahmed, S., Banks, S. and Duce, C. (2007) *Walking Alongside Young People: Challenges and Opportunities for Faith Communities*. Durham: Durham University/The Churches' Regional Commission in the North East.

Aiken, N. (1994) *Working with Teenagers*. London: Marshall Pickering.

Anderson, R., Brown, I., Dowty, T., Heath, W., Inglesant, P. and Sasse, A. (2009) *Database State*. York: Joseph Rowntree Reform Trust.

Armson, A. and Turnbull, S. (1944) *Reckoning with Youth*. London: Allen and Unwin.

Ashton, M. (1986) *Christian Youth Work*. Eastbourne: Kingsway.

Audit Commission (2009) *Tired of Hanging Around: Using Sport and Leisure Activities to Prevent Anti-Social Behaviour by Young People*. London: Audit Commission.

Baden-Powell, R. (1908) *Scouting for Boys: A Handbook for Instruction in Good Citizenship*. London: Horace Cox.

Badham, B. and Davies, T. (2007) 'The Active Involvement of Young People' in R. Harrison, C. Benjamin, S. Curran and R. Hunter (eds) *Leading Work with Young People*. London: Sage.

Banks, S. (1996) 'Youth Work, Informal Education and Professionalisation: The Issues in the 1990s' *Youth and Policy* 54: 13–25.

Banks, S. (1999) *Ethical Issues in Youth Work*. London: Routledge.

Barber, B. R. (1998) *A Place for Us: How to Make Society Civil and Democracy Strong*. New York: Hill and Wang.

Barber, B. R. (2007) *Consumed: How Markets Corrupt Children, Infantilize Adults and Swallow Citizens Whole*. New York: Norton.

Barry, W. A. and Connolly, W. J. (1986) *The Practice of Spiritual Direction*. New York: Harper and Collins.

Barton, A. and Barton, S. (2007) 'Location, Location, Location: The Challenges of "Space" and "Place" in Youth Work Policy' *Youth and Policy* 96: 41–50.

Beck, U. (1992) *Risk Society Towards a New Modernity*. London: Sage.

Beck, U. (2005) *Power in the Global Age*. Cambridge: Polity Press.

Bell, S. and Coleman, S. (1999) 'The Anthropology of Friendship: Enduring Themes and Possibilities' in S. Bell and S. Coleman (eds) *The Anthropology of Friendship*. Oxford: Berg.

171

Bircham, E. and Charlton, J. (2001) *Anti-Capitalism: A Guide to the Movement*. London: Bookmarks.

Blyth, C. (2008) *The Art of Conversation*. London: John Murray.

Boardman, J., Griffin, J. and Murray, O. (1992) *The Oxford History of the Classical World*. Oxford: Oxford University Press.

Bone, M. and Ross, E. (1972) *The Youth Service and Similar Provision for Young People*. London: Stationery Office.

Bradford, S. (2009) 'From Knowledge of the World to Knowledge of Self: Perspectives on the Professional Training of Youth Leaders 1942–1948' in R. Gilchrist, T. Jeffs, J. Spence and J. Walker (eds) *Essays on the History of Youth and Community Work*. Lyme Regis: Russell House Press.

Bradshaw, J. and Mayhew, E. (2005) *The Well-Being of Children in the UK*. London: Save the Children.

Brent, J. (2004) 'Communicating What Youth Work Achieves: The Smile and the Arch' *Youth and Policy* 69: 69–73.

Brew, J. Macalister (1943) *In the Service of Youth: A Practical Manual for Work Among Adolescents?* London: Faber.

Brew, J. Macalister (1946) *Informal Education: Adventures and Reflections*. London: Faber.

Brew, J. Macalister (1949) *Hours Away from Work*. London: National Association of Girls' Clubs and Mixed Clubs.

Brew, J. Macalister (1957) *Youth and Youth Groups*. London: Faber.

Brierley, D. (2003) *Joined Up: An Introduction to Youth Work and Ministry*. Cumbria: Authentic Lifestyle.

Brierley, P. (2000) *The Tide is Running Out*. London: Christian Research.

Brookfield, S. (1983) *Adult Learners, Adult Education, and the Community*. Buckingham: Open University Press.

Brown, S., Heald, M. and Sallans, C. (1995) *Nobody Listens. Problems and Promise for Youth Provision*. Middlesborough: Middlesborough City Challenge and Middlesborough Safer Cities Project.

Buber, M. (2002) *Between Man and Man*. London: Routledge.

Burrell, I. (2000) 'Cambridge Two Will Not Go Back to Prison' *Independent* 2nd December.

Button, L. (1974) *Developmental Group Work with Adolescents*. London: University of London Press. http://www.independent.co.uk/news/UK/crime/cambridge-two-will-not-go-back-to-prison-626464.html. Accessed 11 September 2009.

Callinicos, A. (1999) *Social Theory: A Historical Introduction*. Cambridge: Polity Press.

Cannan, C., Berry, L. and Lyons, K. (1992) *Social Work and Europe*. London: Macmillan.

Carter, P., Jeffs, T. and Smith, M. K. (1995) *Social Working*. London: Macmillan.

Centre for Youth Ministry (2006) *Report of the Christian Youth Work Community Workforce Development Day*. Swindon: Centre for Youth Ministry.

Christian, C. and Kitto, J. (1987) *The Theory and Practice of Supervision*. London: YMCA National College.

Church of England (1996) *Youth A Part*. London: National Society/Church House Publishing.

Clarke, J. and Newman, J. (1997) *The Managerial State*. London: Sage.

Coates, D. (1993) 'Managing Workers' in M. K. Smith (ed.) *Setting Up and Managing Projects*. London: YMCA George Williams College/Rank Foundation.

Coles, B., England, J. and Rugg, J. (1998) *Working with Young People on Estates*. York: Joseph Rowntree Foundation.

Colley, H. (2003) *Mentoring for Social Inclusion*. London: Routledge.

Coombs, P. H. and Ahmed, M. (1974) *Attacking Rural Poverty: How Non-Formal Education Can Help*. Baltimore: John Hopkins University Press.

Coyle, G. L. (1948) *Group Work and American Youth: A Guide to the Practice of Leadership*. New York: Harper and Brothers.

Cray, G. (1998) *Postmodern Culture and Youth Discipleship*. Cambridge: Grove Books.

Crenson, M. (1971) *The Un-Politics of Air Pollution: A Study of Non-Decision Making in the Cities*. Baltimore: John Hopkins University Press.

Cressey, G. (2007) *The Ultimate Separatist Cage? Youth Work with Muslim Young Women*. Leicester: National Youth Agency.

Crimmens, D., Factor, F., Jeffs, T., Pitts, J., Pugh, C., Spence, J. and Turner, P. (2004) *Researching Socially Excluded Young People: A National Study of Street-Based Youth Work*. York: Joseph Rowntree Foundation.

Cruddas, L. (2005) *Learning Mentors in Schools: Policy and Practice*. Stoke-on-Trent: Trentham Books.

Dallow, G. (2002) *Touching the Future*. Oxford: Bible Reading Fellowship.

Darling, N., Hamilton, S. F. and Niego, S. (1994) 'Adolescents' Relations with Adults Outside the Family' in R. Montemayor, G. R. Adams and T. P. Gullotta (eds) *Personal Relationships During Adolescence*. Thousand Oaks, CA: Sage.

Davies, B. (1975) *The Use of Groups in Social Work Practice*. London: Routledge and Kegan Paul.

Davies, B. (2005) 'Youth Work: A Manifesto for Our Times' *Youth and Policy* 88: 5–28.

Davies, B. and Gibson, A. (1967) *The Social Education of the Adolescent*. London: University of London Press.

Davis, M. (2000) *Fashioning a New World: A History of the Woodcraft Folk*. Loughborough: Holyoake Books.

Dee, H. (2004) *Anti-Capitalism: Where Now?* London: Bookmarks.

Department for Education and Employment (1999) *Excellence in Cities*. London: Department for Education and Employment, http://www.standards.dfes.gov.uk/otherresources/publications/excellence/. Accessed 25 September 2005.

Department for Education and Skills (2002) *Transforming Youth Work – Resourcing Excellent Youth Services*. London: Department for Education and Skills/Connexions.

Department of Education and Science (1969) *Youth and Community Work in the 70s* (The Fairbairn-Milson Report). London: HMSO.

Department of Education and Science (1983) *Young People in the 80's: A Survey.* London: HMSO.

Devlin, M. (2008) 'Youth Work and Youth Policy in the Republic of Ireland 1983–2008: "Still haven't found what we're looking for . . .?" ' *Youth and Policy* 100: 41–54.

Dewey, J. (1916) *Democracy and Education: An Introduction to the Philosophy of Education* (1966 edition). New York: Free Press.

Dewey, J. (1963) *Experience and Education*. London: Collier-Macmillan.

Dorling, D., Rigby, J., Wheeler, B., Ballas, D., Thomas, B., Fahmy, E., Gordon, D. and Lupton, R. (2007) *Poverty, Wealth and Place in Britain 1968–2005*. York: Joseph Rowntree Foundation.

Doyle, M. E. (1999) 'Called to Be An Informal Educator' *Youth and Policy* 65: 28–37.

Doyle, M. E. and Smith, M. K. (1999) *Born and Bred? Leadership, Heart and Informal Education*. London: YMCA George Williams College/The Rank Foundation.

Doyle, M. E. and Smith, M. K. (2002) 'Friendship and Informal Education' in *The Encyclopaedia of Informal Education*, http://www.infed.org/biblio/friendship.htm. Accessed 21 September 2007.

Doyle, M. E. and Smith, M. K. (forthcoming) *Christian Youth Work: Legacies and Lessons*. London: YMCA George Williams College/The Rank Foundation.

Drakeford, M. (1998) *Youth Work Practice – Youth Work Training*. Caerphilly: Wales Youth Agency.

Draper, B. and Draper, K. (2000) *Refreshing Worship*. Oxford: Bible Reading Fellowship.

Duck, S. (1998) *Human Relationships*. London: Sage.

Eastman, M. (1976) *Inside Out*. London: Church Pastoral Aid Society (CPAS).

Eastman, D. (2002) *Pathways of Delight*. Ventura, CA: Regal Books.

Edwards-Rees, D. (1943) *The Service of Youth Book*. London: The National Society.

Elsdon, K., Reynolds, J. and Stewart, S. (1995) *Voluntary Organisations: Citizenship, Learning and Change*. Leicester: National Institute of Adult and Continuing Education.

Eraut, M. (1994) *Developing Professional Knowledge and Competence*. London: Flamer Press.

Esmée Fairbairn Foundation/Cambridge University (2007) *The Primary Review: The Condition and Future of Primary Education in England*, http://www.primaryreview.org.uk/index.html. Accessed 1 December 2007.

Feasey, D. (1972) 'Why Activities?' in B. Davies and J. Rogers (eds) *Working with Youth*. London: BBC Publications.

Feinstein, L., Bynner, J. and Duckworth, K. (2006) 'Young People's Leisure Contexts and Their Relation to Adult Outcomes' *Journal of Youth Studies* 9(3): 305–327.

Feinstein, L., Bynner, J. and Duckworth, K. (2007) *Leisure Contexts in Adolescence and Their Associations with Adult Outcomes: A More Complete Picture.* London: Centre for Research on the Wider Benefits of Learning, http://www.learningbenefits.net/Publications/ResReps/ResRep15.pdf. Accessed 21 November 2007.

Ferguson, N. (1982) 'Freire on Education: A Critical Consciousness' *New Education* 4(1): 21–29.

Ford, K., Hunter, R., Merton, B. and Waller, D. (2002) *Transforming Youth Work Management Programme Course Reader.* London: fpm.

Foreman, A. (1987) 'Youth Workers as Redcoats' in T. Jeffs and M. Smith (eds) *Youth Work.* Basingstoke: Macmillan.

Forrest, D. and Wood, S. (1999) 'An Empowering Approach to Working with Young People' *Concept* 9(3): 8–11.

Francis, L. J. and Roberts, M. (2005) *Urban Hope and Spiritual Voice: The Adolescent Voice.* Peterborough: Epworth.

Freedman, M. (1993) *The Kindness of Strangers: Adult Mentors, Urban Youth and the New Volunteerism.* San Francisco: Jossey-Bass.

Freire, P. (1972) *Pedagogy of the Oppressed.* London: Penguin.

Freire, P. (1976) *Education: The Practice of Freedom.* London: Writers and Readers Publishing Co-operative.

Freire, P. (1996) *Pedagogy of Hope: Reliving Pedagogy of the Oppressed.* New York: Continuum Publishing.

Freud, S. (1900) *The Interpretation of Dreams.* London: Hogarth Press.

Fulat, S. and Jaffrey, R. (2006) 'Muslim Youth Helpline: A Model of Youth Engagement in Service Delivery' *Youth and Policy* 92: 151–171.

Furedi, F. (2001) *Paranoid Parenting.* Harmondsworth: Penguin.

Furedi, F. (2005) *Politics of Fear.* London: Continuum.

Furlong, A. and Cartmel, F. (1997) *Young People and Social Change: Individualisation and Risk in Late Modernity.* Buckingham: Open University Press.

Furlong, A., Cartmel, F., Powney, J. and Hall, S. (1997) *Evaluating Youth Work with Vulnerable Young People.* Edinburgh: Scottish Council for Research in Education.

Gaarder, J. (1995) *Sophie's World: A Novel About the History of Philosophy.* London: Phoenix of Orion Books.

Giddens, A. (1990) *The Consequences of Modernity.* Cambridge: Polity Press.

Gillespie, N., Lovett, T. and Garner, W. (1992) *Youth Work and Working Class Youth Culture.* Buckingham: Open University Press.

Gladwell, M. (2000) *The Tipping Point: How Little Things Can Make a Big Difference.* London: Abacus.

Goetschius, G. and Tash, J. (1967) *Working with Unattached Youth.* London: Routledge and Kegan Paul.

Goffman, E. (1969) *The Presentation of Self in Everyday Life.* Harmondsworth: Penguin.

Goleman, D. (1993) *Emotional Intelligence.* London: Bloomsbury.

Gordon, S. (1989) *Balancing Acts; How To Encourage Youth Participation*. Leicester: National Youth Bureau.

Government of Ireland (2001) *Youth Work Act 2001*, http://www.irishstatutebook.ie/2001/en/act/pub/0042/print.html#parti-sec3. Accessed 2 April 2007.

Green, D. and Green, M. (2000) *Taking A Part*. London: National Society/Church House Publishing.

Green, L. (1990) *Let's Do Theology*. London: Mowbray.

Green, M. (2005) *Spirituality and Spiritual Development in Youth Work: A Consultation Paper for the National Youth Agency*. Leicester: National Youth Agency.

Green, M. and Christian, C. (1998) *Accompanying*. London: National Society/Church House Publishing.

Griffith, R. (2000) *National Curriculum? National Disaster?* London: Routledge/Falmer.

Griffin, G. (1993) *Representations of Youth*. Cambridge: Polity Press.

H. M. Government (2005) *Youth Matters*. London: The Stationery Office.

Halpin, D. (2003a) *Hope and Education: The Role of the Utopian Imagination*. London: Routledge-Falmer.

Halpin, D. (2003b) 'Hope, Utopianism and Educational Renewal' in *The Encyclopaedia of Informal Education*, http://www.infed.org/biblio/hope.htm. Updated 17 June 2007.

Hamid, S. (2006) 'Models of Muslim Youthwork: Between Reform and Empowerment' *Youth and Policy* 92: 81–90.

Hanley, L. (2007) *Estates: An Intimate History*. London: Granta Books.

Hargreaves, S. (2002) 'Sexy Supervision' *Young People Now* 155, March.

Harris, J. Rich (1998) *The Nurture Assumption*. New York: Free Press.

Harrison, R., Benjamin, C., Curran, S. and Hunter, R. (2007) *Leading Work with Young People*. London: Sage.

Hay, D. and Nye, R. (1998) *The Spirit of the Child*. London: Harper-Collins.

Hazler, R. J. (1998) *Helping in the Hallways: Advanced Strategies for Enhancing School Relationships*. Thousand Oaks, CA: Corwin Press.

Henriques, B. (1933) *Club Leadership*. London: Oxford University Press.

Hickford, A. (1998) *Essential Youth*. Worthing: Kingsway Publications.

Hirsch, B. J. (2005) *A Place to Call Home: After-School Programs for Urban Youth*. New York: Teachers College Press.

H. M. Government (2003) *Every Child Matters*. London: The Stationery Office.

HM Treasury (2007) *Aiming High for Young People: A Ten Year Strategy for Positive Activities*. London: HM Treasury/Department for Children, Schools and Families.

Hook, S. (2008) 'New Coalition Fights for Adult Students' *Times Educational Supplement* 29 August.

Horton, M. (1990) *The Long Haul*. New York: Doubleday.

Hunt, S. (2004) *The Alpha Enterprise: Evangelism in a Post-Christian Era*. Aldershot: Ashgate.

Huskins, J. (2001) *Quality Work with Young People, Developing Social Skills and Diversion from Risk*. Bristol: Huskins.

Hussain, S. G. (undated) 'Muslim Britain' *Islamic Supreme Council of Canada (ISCC)*, http://www.islamicsupremecouncil.com/muslimbritain.htm. Accessed 24 January 2008.

Illich, I. (1971) *De-Schooling Society*. Harmondsworth: Penguin.

Ingram, G. and Harris, J. (2001) *Delivering Good Youth Work: A Guide to Surviving and Thriving*. Lyme Regis: Russell House Publishing.

Jeffs, A. J. (1979) *Young People and the Youth Service*. London: Routledge and Kegan Paul.

Jeffs, T. (2001) ' "Something to give and much to learn": Settlements and Youth Work' in R. Gilchrist and T. Jeffs (eds) *Settlements, Social Change and Community Action*. London: Jessica Kingsley.

Jeffs, T. (2005a) 'Citizenship, Youth Work and Democratic Renewal' in *The Encyclopaedia of Informal Education*, http://www.infed.org/ association/citizenship_youth_work_democratic_renewal. Accessed 1 December 2008.

Jeffs, T. (2005b) *Newcastle YMCA 150 Years*. Newcastle: Newcastle YMCA.

Jeffs, T. (2007) 'Crossing the Divide: School-Based Youth Work' in R. Harrison, C. Benjamin, S. Curran and R. Hunter (eds) *Leading Work with Young People*. London: Sage.

Jeffs, T. and Smith, M. K. (1990) *Using Informal Education: An Alternative to Casework, Teaching and Control?* Milton Keynes: Open University Press.

Jeffs, T. and Smith, M. K. (2002) 'Individualization and Youth Work' *Youth and Policy* 76: 39–65.

Jeffs, T. and Smith, M. K. (2005) *Informal Education: Conversation, Democracy and Learning*. Nottingham: Educational Heretics Press.

Jeffs, T. and Smith, M. K. (2008) 'Valuing Youth Work' *Youth and Policy* 100: 277–302.

Jeffs, T. and Spence, J. (2008) 'Farewell to All That? The Uncertain Future of Youth and Community Work Education' *Youth and Policy* 97/98: 135–166.

Jenkinson, S. (2002) 'The Importance of Being Supervised' *Young People Now* 161: September.

Johal, R. (2003) *Spirituality in a Multifaith Society*. London: Frontier Youth Trust.

Kadushin, A. and Harness, D. (2002) *Supervision in Social Work* (4th edition). New York: Columbia University Press.

Kane, J. (2003) *How to Heal: A Guide for Caregivers*. New York: Helios Press.

Khan, M. G. (2006) 'Towards a National Strategy for Muslim Youth Work' *Youth and Policy* 92: 7–18.

Kieffer, C. H. (1984) 'Citizen Empowerment: A Developmental Perspective' *Prevention in Human Services* 4(2): 9–36.

Kinast, R. L. (1996) *Let Ministry Teach*. Collegeville, MN: Liturgical Press.

Kinast, R. L. (1999) *Making Faith-sense*. Collegeville, MN: Liturgical Press.

Klein, N. (2000) *No Logo*. London: Flamingo.

Knowles, M. S. (1950) *Informal Adult Education*. New York: Association Press.

Kolb, D. (1976) *The Learning Style Inventory: Technical Manual*. Boston: McBer.

Kolb, D. (1984) *Experiential Learning*. Englewood Cliffs: Prentice Hall.

Konopka, G. (1972) *Social Group Work: A Helping Process* (2nd edition). New York: Prentice-Hall.

Lane, R. E. (2000) *The Loss of Happiness in Market Economies*. New Haven: Yale University Press.

Langford, M. L. (1982) *Unblind Faith*. London: SCM Press.

Laplanche, J. and Pontalis, J. B. (1973) *The Language of Psychoanalysis*. London: Hogarth Press.

Lave, J. and Wenger, E. (1991) *Situated Learning: Legitimate Peripheral Participation*. Cambridge: University of Cambridge Press.

Layard, R. (2005) *Happiness: Lessons from a New Science*. London: Allen Lane.

Lee, J. (1999) *Spiritual Development*. London: United Reform Church (URC).

Levin, P. (1987) *Being Friends*. London: Fount Paperbacks.

Lindeman, E. C. 'The Roots of Democratic Culture' cited in G. Konopka (1972) *Social Group Work: A Helping Process* (2nd edition). New York: Prentice-Hall.

Lloyd, T. (2004) 'Youth Clubs Find It Pays to Grow Your Own Staff' *Young People Now* 248, 1 September.

Loader, B. D. (2007) *Young Citizens in the Digital Age: Political Engagement, Young People and New Media*. London: Routledge.

Lord, J. and Farlow, D. M. (1990) 'A Study of Personal Empowerment: Implications for Health Promotion' *Health Promotion, Health and Welfare* 29(2): 8–15.

Lukes, S. (2005) *Power: A Radical View*. London: Macmillan.

Luxmoore, N. (2000) *Listening to Young People in School, Youth Work and Counselling*. London: Jessica Kingsley.

Mahoney, J. L., Larson, R. W. and Eccles, J. S. (2005) *Organised Activities as Contexts of Development*. Mahwah, NJ: Lawrence Erlbaum Associates.

Mahoney, J. L., Stattin, H. And Magnusson, D. (2001) 'Youth Recreation Center Participation and Criminal Offending: A 20-Year Study of Swedish Boys' *International Journal of Behavioral Development* 25: 509– 520.

Margo, J., Dixon, M., Pearce, N. and Reed, H. (2006) *Freedom's Orphans: Raising Youth in a Changing World*. London: Institute for Public Policy Research.

Marx, K. (1963) 'Economic and Philosophical Manuscripts' in T. B. Bottomore (ed.) *Karl Marx: Early Writings*. Harmondsworth: Penguin.

Marx, K. (1970) 'Theses on Feuerbach' in K. Marx and F. Engels *The German Ideology* edited by C. J. Arthur. London: Lawrence and Wishart.

Marx, K. and Engels, F. (1994) *The German Ideology*. London: Lawrence and Wishart.

Matthews, J. (1966) *Working with Youth Groups*. London: University of London Press.

Mayo, E. and Nairns, A. (2009) *Consumer Kids: How Big Business Is Grooming Our Kids for Profit*. London: Constable.

McAllister, D. (1999) *Saving the Millennial Generation*. Nashville: Thomas Nelson.

McKeown, S. (2006) *Safe as Houses*. London: Shelter.

McKernan, J. (2008) *Curriculum and Imagination: Process Theory, Pedagogy and Action Research*. Abingdon: Routledge.

McLaughlin, M. W., Irby, M. A. and Langman, J. (1994) *Urban Sanctuaries: Neighbourhood Organizations in the Lives of Futures of Inner-City Youth*. San Francisco: Jossey-Bass.

McKnight, J. (1995) *The Careless Society*. New York: Basic Books.

Measor, L. and Squires, P. (2000) *Young People and Community Safety: Inclusion, Risk, Tolerance and Disorder*. Aldershot: Ashgate.

Merton, B. [with contributions by Payne, M. and Smith, D.] (2004) *An Evaluation of the Impact of Youth Work in England (Research Report No. 606)*. London: Department for Education and Skills.

Millar, G. (1995) 'Beyond Managerialism: An Exploration of the Occupational Culture of Youth and Community Work' *Youth and Policy* 50: 49–58.

Mills, C. Wright (1959) *The Sociological Imagination*. New York: Oxford University Press.

Milson, F. W. (1963) *Social Group Method and Christian Education*. London: Chester House.

Milson, F. W. (1982) *Why Am I a Youth Worker: An Examination of the Goals and Motives of Youth Workers*. London: NAYC Publications. Available in *the informal education archives*: http://www.infed.org/archives/nayc/milson_why.htm.

Ministry of Education (1960) *The Youth Service in England and Wales* ('The Albemarle Report'). London: HMSO. Also in the informal education archives, http://www.infed.org/archives/albemarlereport/index.htm.

Montagu, L. (1954) *My Club and I*. London: Neville Spearman and Herbert Joseph.

Montague, C. J. (1904) *Sixty Years in Waifdom: Or, The Ragged School Movement in English History*. London: Charles Murray.

Moore, M. H. (1995) *Creating Public Value: Strategic Management in Government*. Cambridge: Harvard University Press.

Mowat, C. L. (1955) *Britain Between the Wars, 1918–1940*. London: Methuen.

Mulgan, G. with Ali, R., Halkett, R. and Saunders, B. (2007) *In and Out of Sync. The Challenge of Growing Social Innovations*. London: National Endowment for Science Technology and the Arts (NESTA).

Mullender, A. and Ward, D (1991) *Self-Directed Groupwork: Users Take Action for Empowerment*. London: Whiting and Birch.

National Mentoring Network (2000) *Mentoring*. Manchester: National Mentoring Network.

National Youth Agency (2000) *Modern Services for Young People*. Leicester: National Youth Agency.

National Youth Agency (2003) *The NYA Audit: the Basic Facts 2001/2*. Leicester: NYA.

National Youth Agency (2004) *Inter-Faith Consultation Project*. Leicester: NYA.

Newman, E. and Ingram, G. (1989) *The Youth Work Curriculum*. London: Further Education Unit.

Newman, E. and Robertson, S. (2006) 'Leslie Button and the Rise of Developmental Group Work' in R. Gilchrist, T. Jeffs and J. Spence (eds) *Drawing on the Past: Studies in the History of Community and Youth Work*. Leicester: Youth Work Press.

Nicholls, D. (1995) *Employment Practice and Policies in Youth and Community Work*. Lyme Regis: Russell House Publishing.

Nicholls, D. (1999) 'Fairness at Work: The Importance of Supervision' *Young People Now* 125, September.

Office of National Statistics (2006) *Social Trends*. London: HMSO.

Ofsted (2002) *Inspection Reports on Barnet and Manchester Youth Services*. London: Ofsted.

Ofsted (2003) *Inspection of Local Authority Youth Services: Inspection Framework*. London: Ofsted.

Ofsted (2005) *The Framework for Inspection of Children's Services*. London: Ofsted.

Ofsted (2006) *Building on the Best: Overview of Local Authority Youth Services 2005–06*. London: Ofsted.

Ord, J. (2004) 'The Youth Work Curriculum and the "Transforming Youth Work Agenda" ' *Youth and Policy* 83: 43–59.

Ord, J. (2007) *Youth Work Process, Product and Practice: Creating an Authentic Curriculum in Work with Young People*. Lyme Regis: Russell House.

Osgood, D. W., Anderson, A. L. and Shaffer, J. N. (2005) 'Unstructured Leisure in the After-School Hours' in J. L. Mahoney, R. W. Larson and J. S. Eccles (eds) *Organized Activities as Contexts of Development: Extracurricular Activities After-School and Community Programs*. Mahwah, NJ: Lawrence Erlbaum Associates.

Osgood, D. W., Wilson, J. K., O'Malley, P. M., Bachman, J. G. and Johnston, L. D. (1996) 'Routine Activities and Individual Deviant Behaviour' *American Sociological Review* 61: 635–655.

Pahl, R. (2000) *On Friendship*. Cambridge: Polity Press.

Palmer, P. J. (1997) 'The Heart of a Teacher: Identity and Integrity in Teaching' *Change Magazine* 29(6): 14–21, November/December, found at http://www.mcli.dist.maricopa.edu/events/afc99/articles/heartof.html.

Palmer, P. J. (1998) *The Courage to Teach: Exploring the Inner Landscape of a Teacher's Life*. San Francisco: Jossey-Bass.

Paneth, M. (1944) *Branch Street*. London: Allen and Unwin.

PAULO (2002) *National Occupational Standards for Youth Work*. London: PAULO NTO.

Payne, M. (2005) 'Working with Groups' in R. Harrison and C. Wise (eds) *Working with Young People*. London: Sage.

Perls, F. S. (1947) *Ego, Hunger and Aggression*. London: Allen and Unwin.

Philip, K. (2000) 'Mentoring: Pitfalls and Potential for Young People' *Youth and Policy* 67: 1–15.

Philip, K. (2008) 'Youth Mentoring – A Case for Treatment' *Youth and Policy* 99: 17–32.

Pimlott, N. (2001) *Faiths and Frontiers*. Birmingham: Frontier Youth Trust.

Power, A. (2007) *City Survivors: Bringing Up Children in Disadvantaged Neighbourhoods*. Bristol: Policy Press.

Power, A. and Tunstall, R. (1995) *Swimming Against the Tide: Polarisation and Progress on Twenty Unpopular Council Estates 1980–95*. York: JRF.

Putnam, R. D. (1993) *Making Democracy Work: Civic Traditions in Modern Italy*. Princeton: Princeton University Press.

Putnam, R. D. (2000) *Bowling Alone: The Collapse and Revival of American Community*. New York: Simon and Schuster.

Ranson, S. and Stewart, J. (1994) *Management for the Public Domain: Enabling the Learning Society*. Basingstoke: Macmillan.

Rappaport, J. (1981) 'In Praise of Paradox' *American Journal of Community Psychology* 9: 1–25.

Rappaport, J., Swift, C. and Hess, R. (1984) *Studies in Empowerment: Steps Toward Understanding and Action*. New York: Haworth.

Rayner, E. (1986) *Human Development* (3rd edition). London: Allen and Unwin.

Reed, B. (1950) *Eighty Thousand Adolescents: A Study of Young People in Birmingham*. London: Allen and Unwin.

Rees, D. M. M. E. (1943) *The Service of Youth Book*. Wallington: Religious Education Press.

Rees, D. M. M. E. (1944) *A Rural Youth Service: Suggestions for Youth Work in the Countryside*. Wallington: Religious Education Press.

Reid, K. E. (1981) *From Character Building to Social Treatment: The History of Groups in Social Work*. Westport, CO: Greenwood Press.

Rhodes, J. (1994) 'Older and Wiser – Mentoring Relationships in Childhood and Adolescence' *Journal of Primary Prevention* 14: 187–196.

Rhodes, J. (2002) *Stand by Me: The Risks and Rewards of Mentoring Today's Youth*. Cambridge: Harvard University Press.

Rhodes, J. and Lowe, S. R. (2008) 'Youth Mentoring: Improving Programmes Through Research-Based Practice' *Youth and Policy* 99: 9–16.

Richardson, E. (2008) *DIY Community Action: Neighbourhood Problems and Community Self-Help*. Bristol: Policy Press.

Riley, P. (2001) 'Programme Planning' in L. Deer Richardson and M. Wolfe (eds) *Principles and Practice of Informal Education*. London: Routledge Falmer.

Robb, M., Barrett, S., Komaromy, C. and Rogers, A. (2004) *Communication, Relationship and Care: A Reader*. London: Routledge.

Robertson, S. (2000) 'A Warm, Safe Place: An Argument for Youth Clubs' *Youth and Policy* 70: 71–78.

182 | References

Robertson, S. (2005) *Youth Clubs: Association, Participation, Friendship and Fun.* Lyme Regis: Russell House Publishing.

Rogers, C. (2001) *The Carl Rogers Reader*, H. Kirschenbaum and V. L. Henderson (eds). London: Constable.

Rose, C. (1998) *Touching Lives: A Personal History of Clapton Jewish Youth Centre.* Leicester: Youth Work Press.

Rosseter, B. (1987) 'Youth Workers as Educators' in T. Jeffs and M. Smith (eds) *Youth Work.* Basingstoke: Macmillan.

Russell, C. E. B. (1932) *Lads' Clubs: Their History, Organisation and Management.* London: A. C. Black.

Sacks, J. (2002) *The Dignity of Difference.* London: Continuum.

Savage, J. (2007) *Teenage: The Creation of Youth Culture.* London: Viking.

Scales, P. C., Benson, P. L. and Roehlkepartain, E. C. (2001) *Grading Grown-Ups: American Adults Report on Their Real Relationships with Kids.* Minneapolis: Lutheran Brotherhood and Search Institute.

Schön, D. (1983) *The Reflective Practitioner: How Professionals Think in Action.* New York: Basic Books.

Schön, D. (1987) *Educating the Reflective Practitioner.* San Francisco: Jossey-Bass.

Scott, A. (1990) *Ideology and the New Social Movements.* London: Routledge.

Scottish Executive (2003) *Working and Learning Together to Build Stronger Communities: Draft Community Learning and Development Guidance.* Edinburgh: The Scottish Executive.

Scottish Executive (2007) *Moving Forward: A Strategy for Improving Young People's Chances Through Youth Work.* Edinburgh: The Scottish Executive.

Senge, P. (1990) *The Fifth Discipline: The Art and Practice of the Learning Organization.* New York: Random House.

Sennett, R. (2006) *The Culture of the New Capitalism.* New Haven: Yale University Press.

Sherman, N. (1997) *Making a Necessity of Virtue.* Cambridge: Cambridge University Press.

Shiner, M., Young, T., Newburn, T. and Groben, S. (2004) *Mentoring Disaffected Young People: An Evaluation of 'Mentoring Plus'.* York: JRF.

Siranni, C. and Friedland, L. (2001) *Civic Innovation in America: Community Empowerment, Public Policy and the Movement for Civic Renewal.* Berkeley: University of California Press.

Smith, H. and Smith, M. K. (2008) *The Art of Helping Others. Being Around, Being There, Being Wise.* London: Jessica Kingsley.

Smith, M. K. (1994) *Local Education: Community, Conversation, Praxis.* Buckingham: Open University Press.

Smith, M. K. (1999, 2009) 'Social Pedagogy' in *The Encyclopaedia of Informal Education*, http://www.infed.org/biblio/b-socped.htm. Accessed 22 March 2009.

Smith, M. K. (2001a) 'Young People, Informal Education and Association' *The Informal Education Homepage*, http://www.infed.org/ youthwork/ypandassoc.htm. Accessed 11 October 2008.

Smith, M. K. (2001b) 'Josephine Macalister Brew' in R. Gilchrist, T. Jeffs and J. Spence (eds) *Essays in the History of Community and Youth Work*. Leicester: Youth Work Press.

Smith, M. K. (2002a) 'Globalization and the Incorporation of Education' in *The Encyclopaedia of Informal Education*, http://www.infed.org/biblio/globaliza tion.htm. Accessed 22 March 2009.

Smith, M. K. (2002b) 'Transforming Youth Work – Resourcing Excellent Youth Services: A Critique' in *The Encylopaedia of Informal Education*, http://www.infed.org/youthwork/transforming_youth_work_2, htm. Accessed 22 March 2009.

Smith, M. K. (2005) 'The Functions of Supervision' in *The Encyclopaedia of Informal Education*, http://www.infed.org/biblio/b-socped.htm. Accessed 22 November 2008.

Smith, W. C. (1962) *The Meaning and Ending of Religion*. New York: Macmillan.

Spence, J. and Devanney, C. with Noonan, K. (2007) *Youth Work: Voices of Practice – A Research Report by Durham University and Weston Spirit*. Leicester: National Youth Agency, http://www.nya.org.uk/Shared_ASP_ Files/UploadedFiles/3A711D1E-6D69-4326-800A-59D4BC62BA40_Voices ofPractice.pdf. Accessed 29 November 2007.

Speth, J. G. (2005) *Red Sky at Morning: America and the Crisis of the Global Environment*. New Haven: Yale University Press.

Stenhouse, L. A. (1980) 'Product or Process? A Reply to Brian Crittenden' reprinted in J. Ruddock and D. Hopkins (1985) *Research as a Basis for Teaching*. London: Heinemann.

Stringer, E. T. (1999) *Action Research*. London: Sage.

Strommer, M., Jones, K. and Rahn, D. (2001) *Youth Ministry that Transforms*. Grand Rapids, MI: Zondervan.

Stuart, G. (2006) 'What Does Gandhi Have to Say About Youth Work?' *Youth and Policy* 93: 77–90.

Tash, M. Joan (2000) *Supervision in Youth Work*. London: George Williams YMCA College.

Taylor, J. V. (1971) *Face to Face, Essays on Inter-Faith Dialogue*. Oxford: Highway Press.

Taylor, T. (1987) 'Youth Workers as Character Builders: Constructing a Socialist Alternative' in T. Jeffs and M. Smith (eds) *Youth Work*. London: Macmillan.

Thatcher, A. (1990) *Truly a Person: Truly God*. London: SPCK.

Thatcher, A. (1999) *Spirituality and the Curriculum*. London: Cassell.

The Salvation Army (2001) *The Burden of Youth*. London: The Henley Centre.

Thompson, N. (2007) 'Using Supervision' in R. Harrison, C. Benjamin, S. Curran and R. Hunter (eds) *Leading Work with Young People*. London: Sage.

Tiffany, G. (2001) 'Relationships and Learning' in L. Deer Richardson and M. Wolfe (eds) *Principles and Practice of Informal Education*. London: Routledge Falmer.

Tocqueville, A. de (1848) *Democracy in America* (translated G. Lawrence 1966). New York: Harper Row.

184 | References

Topping, K. (1996) 'Reaching Where Adults Cannot – Peer Education and Peer Counselling' *Educational Psychology in Practice* 11(4): 23–29.

Tyler, M. (2001) 'Developing Professional Practice' in L. Deer Richardson and M. Wolfe (eds) *Principles and Practice of Informal Education*. London: Routledge Falmer.

UNICEF (2007) *Report Card 7, Child Poverty in Perspective: An Overview of Child Well-Being in Rich Countries*. Florence: UNICEF Innocenti Research Centre, http://www.unicef-icdc.org/presscentre/presskit/reportcard7/rc7_eng.pdf. Accessed 3 November 2008.

Valentine, G. (2004) *Public Space and the Culture of Childhood*. Aldershot: Ashgate.

Vangelisti, A. L. and Perlman, D. (eds) (2006) *The Cambridge Handbook of Personal Relationships*. New York: Cambridge University Press.

Waiton, S. (2008) *The Politics of Antisocial Behaviour*. London: Routledge.

Wales Youth Agency (2002) *The Youth Work Curriculum Statement for Wales*. Caerphilly: Wales Youth Agency.

Walker, J. (1943) 'A Free Programme in the Club' reprinted in D. Rees-Edwards *The Service of Youth Book*. London: The National Society.

Wallerstein, N. (1993) 'Empowerment and Health: The Theory and Practice of Community Change' *Community Development Journal* 28(3): 218–227.

Wanless, D., Appleby, J. and Harrison, A. (2007) *Our Future Health Secured? A Review of NHS Funding and Performance*. London: King's Fund, http://www.kingsfund.org.uk/publications/kings_fund_publications/our_future.html. Accessed 13 September 2007.

Ward, P. (1997) *Youth Work and the Mission of God*. London: SPCK.

Warde, A., Savage, M., Longhurst, B., Tomlinson, M., Ray, K. and Tampubolon, G. (2004) *Brief Report on the Project: Social Capital and Social Networks*, http://www.les1.man.ac.uk/cric/Alan_Warde/pdfs/social.pdf. Accessed 10 October 2004.

Wardhaugh, R. (1985) *How Conversation Works*. Oxford: Basil Blackwell.

Welsh Assembly Government (2007) *Young People, Youth Work, Youth Service. National Youth Service Strategy for Wales*. Cardiff: Welsh Assembly Government.

Wenger, E. (1998) *Communities of Practice: Learning, Meaning and Identity*. Cambridge: Cambridge University Press.

Wenger, E. (2005) 'Communities of Practice: A Brief Introduction' *Etienne Wenger Homepage*, http//www.ewenger.com/theory/index.htm. Accessed 22 March 2009.

Westerhoff, I. (1980) *Will Our Children Have Faith?* New York: Seabury Publishing.

Wilkinson, R. and Pickett, K. (2009) *The Spirit Level: Why More Equal Societies Almost Always Do Better*. London: Allen Lane.

Williamson, H. (2004) *The Milltown Boys Revisited*. Oxford: Berg.

Wilson, P. (1985) *Gutter Feelings: Christian Youth Work in Urban Settings*. London: Marshall Pickering.

Wood, S. and Forrest, D. (2000) 'Participatory Action Research: An Empowering Methodology for Work with Marginalised Young People' *Scottish Youth Issues* 1(1): 63–86.

Woods, J. (2001) 'Using Supervision for Professional Development' in L. Deer Richardson and M. Wolfe (eds) *Principles and Practice of Informal Education: Learning Through Life*. London: Routledge/Falmer.

Young Brown, M. (1983) *The Unfolding Self*. Bayfield, CA: Psychosynthesis Press.

Young, K. (2006) *The Art of Youth Work* (2nd edition). Lyme Regis: Russell House.

Youth Justice Board (2003) *0–19 (ZeroNinteen)*. London: Youth Justice Board.

Index